Teacher Training

Published by
Lotus Press Publishers & Distributors

Teacher Training

Dr. Suraj Prakash Bhan

4735/22, Prakash Deep Building,
Ansari Road, Daryaganj,
New Delhi - 110002

Lotus Press : Publishers & Distributors
Unit No. 220, 2nd Floor, 4735/22, Prakash Deep Building,
Ansari Road, Darya Ganj, New Delhi- 110002
Ph.: 32903912, 23280047, 9811838000
E-mail : lotus_press@sify.com

Teacher Training

ISBN: 81-8382-104-9

Published by : **Lotus Press Publishers & Distributors,** New Delhi-110002
Printed At : **A.J Book Binding House,** New Delhi

PREFACE

Teacher training is an integral component of the educational system. It is intimately connected with society and is conditioned by the ethos, culture and character of a nation. The constitutional goals, the directive principles of the state policy, the socio-economic problems and the growth of knowledge, the emerging expectations and the changes operating in education, etc. call for an appropriate response from a futuristic education system and provide the perspective within which teacher education programmes need to be viewed.

Teacher training can no longer remain conventional and static but should transform itself to a progressive dynamic and responsive system. National values and goals need to be meaningfully reflected and their inculcation attempted with care and caution. The theoretical and practical components need to be balanced appropriately. The theory and practice of education has to be enriched with the latest research findings not only in the field of education but also in the allied disciplines and areas. While it is essential to develop identified competencies to prepare effective teachers, it is equally necessary to develop commitment and build capacity to perform as integral part of teacher preparation.

The teachers have to keep abreast of the latest developments not only in their field of specialisation but also in areas of educational developments and social and cultural issues through continuous in-service orientation. Emphasis on continuing life-long learning has to become an essential concern of teacher education. A nation concerned with erosion of values needs teachers who are professionally committed and prepared to present a value-based model of interaction with their learners. Information highways, websites and internet are going to become terms of common usage in teacher education. For sound mind we need strong hand and a vibrant heart. Areas like physical education and vocational education will continue to gain greater emphasis in years to come and will serve as the basis for developing competencies and skills in addition to commitments and values.

A comprehensive theoretical base is essential for a teacher to assume professional role and develop capacity to conceptualise inputs from other disciplines as well and evolve strategies to utilise them. A true professional is capable of perceiving complexities and uncertainties in the society, has a thorough grasp of the subject, possesses skills to make critical diagnosis, takes decisions and has courage and conviction to implement such decisions.

This book addresses various aspects of teacher training in a sharp and pin-pointed manner. Topics such as context of teacher training, teaching strategies, pre-service teacher training, in-service teacher training, role of ICTs in teacher training, training of women teachers, teacher educator training, value orientation in teacher training, methods of teachers training etc., have been dealt in a very impressive way. It is hoped that this book will prove useful to student-teachers, teaching departments and institutions, teachers of educational administrations and all those concerned.

Editor

CONTENTS

1

CHANGING CONTEXT OF TEACHER TRAINING

Teacher education is intimately connected with society and is conditioned by the ethos, culture and character of a nation. Enlightened teachers lead communities and nations in their march towards better and higher quality of life. They reveal and elaborate the secrets of attaining higher values in life and nurture empathy for the fellow beings. No nation can even marginally slacken its efforts in giving necessary professional inputs to its teachers and along with that due status to their stature and profession.

The quality of education is a direct consequence and outcome of the quality of teachers and teacher education system. The task of bringing qualitative change in institutional efficacy of the teacher education system in itself is a huge and challenging one. The last five decades have witnessed several attempts to change, modify and indigenise the inherited system of teacher education. The system however continues to function more or less on the same principles, similar content and approaches characterised by continuity and unwillingness to change. Over the years the magnitude of the task has increased manifold.

In India, the constitutional goals, the directive principles of the state policy, the socio-economic problems and the growth of knowledge, the emerging expectations and the changes operating in education, etc. call for an appropriate response from a futuristic education system and provide the perspective within which teacher education programmes need to be viewed. When India attained freedom, the then existing educational system was accepted as such because it was thought that an abrupt departure from the same would be disturbing and destabilising. Thus a predisposition to retain the system acquired preponderance and all that was envisaged by way of changes was its rearrangement. Consequently, education including teacher education largely remained isolated from the needs and aspirations of the people. During the last five decades certain efforts have been made to indigenise the system. The gaps, however, are still wide and visible.

The need for improved levels of educational participation for overall progress is well recognised. The key role of educational institutions in realising it is reflected in a variety of initiatives taken to transform the nature and function of education— both formal as well as non-formal. Universal accessibility to quality education is considered essential for development. This has necessitated improvement in the system of teacher education so as to prepare quality teachers.

Various Commissions and Committees appointed by the Central and the State Governments in recent decades have invariably emphasised the need for quality teacher education suited to the needs of the educational system. The Secondary Education Commission (1953) observed that a major factor responsible for the educational reconstruction at the secondary stage is teachers' professional training. The Education Commission (1964-66) stressed that 'in a world based on science and technology it is education that determines the level of prosperity, welfare and security of the people' and that 'a sound programme of professional education of teachers is essential for the qualitative improvement of education.'

In India, there are nearly 5.98 lakh Primary Schools, 1.76 lakh Elementary Schools and 98000 High or Higher Secondary Schools in the country, about 1300 teacher education institutions for elementary teachers and nearly 700 colleges of education/university departments preparing teachers for secondary and higher secondary schools. Out of about 4.52 million teachers in the country nearly 3 million are teaching at the primary/elementary level. A sizeable number of them are untrained or under-trained. In certain regions, like the North-East, there are even under-qualified teachers.

As far as in-service education is concerned the situation is not very encouraging. It is estimated that on an average 40% of the teachers are provided in-service teacher education once over a period of five years. Regarding non-formal education, though a number of models are in vogue in various states in the country, much more needs to be done to prepare teachers and other functionaries for the system.

The Programme of Action (POA 1992) has emphasised teacher education as a continuous process, its pre-service and in-service components being inseparable. The POA, among others, has pointed out the following in respect of teacher education:

— Professional commitment and overall competencies of teachers leave much to be desired;

— The quality of pre-service education has not only not improved with recent developments in pedagogical science, but has actually shown signs of deterioration;

— Teacher education programmes consist mainly of pre-service teacher training, with practically no systematic programmes of inservice training, facilities for which are lacking.

— There has been an increase in sub-standard institutions of teacher education and there are numerous reports of gross malpractices; and

— The support system provided by the State Councils of Educational Research and Training (SCERTs) and the University Departments of Education has been insufficient and there is no support system below the state level.

In pursuance of the NPE 1986 a major step was taken by the Central Government to enhance the professional capacity of a large number of teacher education institutions. Nearly 430 District Institutes of Education and Training (DIETs) have already been established by 1997-98.

The DIETs are charged with the responsibility of organising pre-service and in-service programmes in addition to being the nodal resource centres for elementary education at district level. Likewise, Colleges of Teacher Education (CTEs) and Institutions of Advanced Study in Education (IASEs) have been given the responsibility of introducing innovations in teacher education programmes at the secondary and higher secondary stages and in vocational education.

The National Council for Teacher Education (NCTE) as a non-statutory body (1973-1993) took several steps as regards quality improvement in teacher education. Its major contribution was to prepare Teacher Education Curriculum Framework in 1978. Consequently, teacher education curricula witnessed changes in teacher preparation programmes in various universities and boards in the country. A similar effort was made in 1988.

During the last decade, new thrusts have been posed due to rapid changes in the educational, political, social and economic contexts at the national and international levels. Curriculum reconstruction has also become imperative in the light of some perceptible gaps in teacher education.

Teacher education by and large, is conventional in its nature and purpose. The integration of theory and practice and consequent curricular response to the requirements of the school system still remains inadequate. Teachers are prepared in competencies and skills which do not necessarily equip them for becoming professionally effective. Their familiarity with latest educational developments remains insufficient.

Organised and stipulatory learning experiences whenever available, rarely contribute to enhancing teachers' capacities for self-directed life long learning. The system still prepares teachers who do not necessarily become professionally competent and committed at the completion of initial teacher preparation programmes. A large number of teacher training institutions do not practice what they preach. Several of the skills acquired and methodologies learnt are seldom practiced in actual school system.

GOALS OF TEACHER EDUCATION

The Indian Constitution resolves to constitute India into a sovereign, socialist, secular and democratic republic and secure to all its citizens: justice-social, economic and political; liberty of thought, expression, faith, belief and worship; equality of status and of opportunity; and to promote among them all fraternity assuring the dignity of the individual and the integrity of the nation. These are the main goals which the nation expects to be realised through education. Teacher preparation must not lose sight of this basic thrust so as to empower teachers to inculcate the same among the students.

In order to reinforce faith in democratic socialism, secularism, justice, liberty, freedom etc. the role of education needs to be understood in its true perspective. Democracy is a process of building consensus among the citizens on matters of common concern. It expects high morality from them, protects the interest and preserves their uniqueness, dignity and individuality. Quality of democracy depends on its citizens willing to discharge their responsibilities towards the self, the family, the community, the nation and humanity at large.

Democracy is a way of life and its values need to be imbibed through education and practised in the day-to-day life. Democratic socialism attempts to achieve a synthesis between individual freedom and social compulsion and combines liberty with responsibility and authority with accountability. The Indian situation demands citizens capable of making conscious and purposive efforts directed towards social cohesion and living together harmoniously.

The imposition of a homogeneous and uniform curriculum of teacher education may prove counter productive under this situation. Except for identifying certain basics and essentials, regional autonomy must be exercised for developing region/culture specific curriculum of teacher education. Indian reality demands that plurality should be used for strengthening national solidarity and social cohesion. The Indian state is secular. The Indian society, however, is religious. To resolve this dichotomy between the state and polity, the principle of equal respect for all the religions has been accepted. This is the essence of Indian secularism. The teachers themselves have to internalise the imperatives of secularism in national context and interpret the same effectively to the learners. That alone would develop the right attitudes among all citizens irrespective of their own backgrounds.

Justice, liberty, equality of status and of opportunity and promoting fraternity constitute another set of inter-related goals. Justice protects the rights of the weak and ensures impartiality. To ensure justice and fulfil the constitutional commitments in this regard, certain positive and legal provisions have been made by the state. Special measures such as reservation in educational institutions, financial support, scholarships, hostel facilities, etc. have been extended to the under-privileged groups like Scheduled Castes, Scheduled Tribes, Other Backward Classes etc. It implies change in attitudes and values through education, in which the role of teachers needs to be stressed. Liberty of thought, expression, faith, belief and worship is another constitutional goal which education is expected to help realise.

Indian Constitution ensures equality of status and opportunity to all its citizens. The objective is to minimise social and economic disparities, inequality of power and life chances by positive discrimination in favour of the weak. The education of teachers should equip them with the competencies needed to deal with discrimination, disparities and inequalities. Fraternity stands for acceptance of universal brotherhood, respect for human personality and feeling of oneness irrespective of linguistic, racial, cultural and religious diversities.

ISSUES IN TEACHER EDUCATION

Education is an effective means for social reconstruction and to a great extent it offers solutions to the problems a society is faced with. These problems may be economic, social, cultural, political, moral, ecological and educational. Since the teachers play a major role in education of children, their own education becomes a matter of vital concern.

Education of teachers needs to strengthen and stress upon the main attributes of a profession, such as, the systematic theory, rigourous training over a specified duration, authority, community sanction, ethical code and culture, generating knowledge through research and specialisation. It is acknowledged that formal professional training on continuous basis is necessary for becoming a good teacher as it caters to the development of one's personality and sharpening of communication skills and commitment to a code of conduct.

Economic Issues

Poverty, unemployment, and low rate of growth and productivity are some of the major economic problems of the country which have led to the compulsions of the backward economy. These problems seek immediate solution and demand a realistic co-ordination between economic planning and manpower planning. Education can help find solutions if it is properly coordinated with manpower needs. Introduction of work education and vocationalisation of education in secondary schools will have to be given a modern and meaningful direction. The attitude towards the work culture needs a transformation.

The Indian society needs education with special emphasis on science and technology, vocational inputs and realistic work experiences. Teacher education curriculum, therefore, has to promote such attitudes as are necessary for the emergence of a new economic order. Alongwith the vocational competencies and skills a new work culture will have to be created which necessarily involves the inculcation of dignity of work, the spirit of self-reliance and scientific temper among students. The courses of teacher education need to be enriched to enable teachers to understand the attributes of modernity and development.

Social Problems

Casteism, communalism and regionalism are some of the problems in the body politic of the society which misguide the youth. Increasing delinquency, violence, terrorism and fissiparous tendencies and use of inappropriate means to get one's ends served are threats to the national integration and social cohesion. Democracy, violence and terrorism cannot coexist. Education has to develop a peace loving personality and the programme of teacher education has to contribute in this regard.

The explosion of population with all its allied disturbing trends is not only neutralising the economic gains but also creating many problems for the country. Indian society still suffers from evils like child labour, child marriage, untouchability, discriminatory treatment to women, violation of human rights, etc. and most of the people are unaware of their legal rights. Modern model of development which puts man against nature by making it an object of exploitation has disturbed the harmony and equilibrium between the two. Its consequences are visible in serious environmental degradation, pollution and ecological imbalances.

Strengthening national and social cohesion in a diverse and plural society, accelerating the process of economic growth, improving the life of the downtrodden and the people living below the poverty line, removing the widely prevalent ignorance, superstition and prejudices from the masses, inculcating scientific temper and developing a critical awareness about the social realities of Indian life are some of the issues which call for immediate attention. Teachers and the teacher educators have a special role to play in such efforts.

Cultural Issues

Education is the process of transmission of dynamic and responsive components of cultural heritage and its continuous enrichment. There is a need to reinterpret the Indian culture in its distinct identity and composite strength. Its capacity to absorb the sublime from the other cultures needs to be highlighted. The teachers will have to play their role in cultural transmission and reconstruction.

Issues of Morality

In the present day context certain values need to be redefined and reinstalled. There are situations when the values imparted and inculcated in schools are not generally practised in society. Value education demands a planned and purposive approach. It is through education and as of necessity through teacher education programmes that the task of inculcating values can be substantially accomplished.

Whereas values are emotive, the other related significant dimension is that of moral education which is essentially conative in character. Morals are situation-specific and demand immediate decision and action and yet there are morals which are considered to be eternal and universal. Through committed teachers, the art of ensuring moral development in a secular, multi-religious and multi-ethnic society needs to be cultivated.

Isolation of Teacher Education

Teacher education institutions which were considered 'islands of isolation' have gradually developed linkages with schools, peer institutions, universities and other institutions of higher learning as also the community. However, much remains to be done in this direction. The curriculum of the school, its actual transactional modalities, examination system, management processes and its ethos need to be the main thrust areas of teacher education programmes. To achieve these ends, teacher educators need to be made conversant with various aspects of school experiences.

It is observed in day-to-day functioning that teacher educators often tend to lose contact with content areas relevant to their own disciplines resulting into gaps in communication and latest information. It is, therefore, a felt need in the present-day context that teacher education institutions keep in continuous touch with institutions of higher learning and peer institutions for effective transmission of knowledge and its upgradation.

The breaking of isolation from the community is essential for enabling teachers and teacher educators to reconstruct pedagogical and educational principles and practices in the light of experiences gained from mutually beneficial community interactions. Teacher as a professional and intellectual cannot remain indifferent to the events that are taking place in society. The academic and social issues are inter-related and inter-dependent. In contemporary context, the role of the teacher is no longer confined to teaching alone. The teachers are expected to play an active role in the developmental activities responding to progress of the community.

FUNCTIONS OF TEACHER EDUCATION INSTITUTIONS

In the light of context and concerns teacher education institutions will acquire a wider spectrum of functions and greater responsibilities. Resolution of specific functions from the spectrum will have to be made depending upon the institutional capabilities. It is visualised that the following institutional functions will have to be undertaken by different institutions according to availability of resources:

— develop capability to provide for both pre-service and in-service education.

— provide training and orientation programmes to the functionaries of alternative educational strategies aimed at achieving universal elementary education and eradication of illiteracy.

— organise programmes for heads of schools and school complexes and supervisory staff.

— offer courses for community leaders, voluntary agencies and parents.

— provide academic support to schools and other agencies engaged in education of children and adults.

— undertake research and experiments with innovative educational ideas.

— act as a resource centre for education for a specific area.

— offer counselling and guidance services.

— organise need-based programmes for educational administrators, planners, curriculum designers, evaluators etc.

— impart training for other areas of education, like physical education and special education.

— act as a link between the school and the university system.

COMPETENCY IN TEACHER EDUCATION

A major concern in education is the quality and relevance of education being imparted to learners. Every learner is supposed to acquire mastery level learning in identified competency areas. To enhance the quality of education equal emphasis needs to be given to competencies, commitment and willingness to perform. A curriculum framework based upon competencies, commitments and performance has been developed. Competency areas namely, contextual competencies, conceptual, content, transactional, related to other educational activities, developing teaching learning material, evaluation, management, working with parents and working with community and other agencies, have been identified as critical to teacher preparation at elementary stage.

Acquisition of competencies alone will not be sufficient until and unless the teacher is fully committed. Teacher commitment areas identified include commitment to the learner, commitment to the society, commitment to the profession, commitment to attaining excellence for professional actions and commitment to basic values. Alongwith competency and commitment areas, performance areas have also been identified. These include classroom performance, school level performance, performance in the out-of school educational activities, parents related performance and community related performance.

Teacher education institutions could identify details in each of the three major categories. For each competency, commitment and performance area, the existing curriculum needs to be analysed. Whenever certain unit of curriculum is taken up for transaction, its relationship to commitment and performance has to be examined. Such an approach would provide an opportunity to the training institutions to prepare teachers who are not only competent but also committed and both these aspects are reflected in their performance leading to higher learning attainments by all children.

EXPANDING SCOPE OF TEACHER EDUCATION

Teacher education has to be conceived as an integral part of educational and social system and must primarily respond to the requirements of the school system. It can no longer remain conventional and static but should transform itself to a progressive dynamic and responsive system. National values and goals need to be meaningfully reflected and their inculcation attempted with care and caution. The theoretical and practical components need to be balanced appropriately.

The theory and practice of education has to be enriched with the latest research findings not only in the field of education but also in the allied disciplines and areas. While it is essential to develop identified competencies to prepare effective teachers it is equally necessary to develop commitment and build capacity to perform as integral part of teacher preparation.

The teachers have to keep abreast of the latest developments not only in their field of specialisation but also in areas of educational developments and social and cultural issues through continuous inservice orientation. Emphasis on continuing life-long learning has to become an essential concern of teacher education. A nation concerned with erosion of values needs teachers who are professionally committed and prepared to present a value-based model of interaction with their learners. The basic tenets identified in the national basic education scheme - Head, Heart and Hand need now to be linked to another 'H' - highways. Information highways, websites and internet are going to become terms of common usage in teacher education. For sound mind we need strong hand and a vibrant heart. Areas like physical education and vocational education will continue to gain greater emphasis in years to come and will serve as the basis for developing competencies and skills in addition to commitments and values.

A comprehensive theoretical base is essential for a teacher to assume professional role and develop capacity to conceptualise inputs from other disciplines as well and evolve strategies to utilise them. A true professional is capable of perceiving complexities and uncertainties in the society, has a thorough grasp of the subject, possesses skills to make critical diagnosis, takes decisions and has courage and conviction to implement such decisions.

Education of teachers is not an end in itself. Its target is the school. Any change in the nature, purpose, quality and character of the school demands a concomitant change in teacher education, specially in its curriculum. The implementation of the 10 + 2 scheme at the school level has transformed the complexion of education to a considerable extent from the pre-primary to the + 2 stage. There has been an increase not only in the quantum of knowledge, but also in its nature and purpose.

In addition, new transactional techniques and strategies have also been evolved. Certain new subjects have replaced the old ones whereas some others have changed their context, content, orientation, theme and philosophy. These changes at the school level, out of necessity, demand a new pedagogy and evaluation techniques. But the changes at the level of teacher education have not adequately responded to the emerging realities at the school level. All that the teachers are expected to do in their work places need to be reflected in the teacher education activities and programmes.

The teaching community has to face the challenges thrown by science and technology. There has been an explosion not only of scientific and technological knowledge but also in the means and techniques of acquiring knowledge. The scientific researches and developments related to theories of heredity, learning, mental health, neurology, attention, motivation etc. can no longer be treated alien to teacher education programmes.

Every region and state has its typical cultural identity, and there is a need to utilise the same as a basis for developing meaningful, relevant pedagogies. Since there is no one universal way in which the children learn, there is a strong need for looking into the cultural context in which a child is placed. A child in a tribal society may process information in an altogether different manner as compared to the one from the urban area and high socio-economic stratum. Pedagogy, therefore, should be culture-specific.

Cultural practices such as story-telling, dramatics, puppetry, folk-play, community living, etc. should become a strong basis of pedagogy instead of using one uniform, mechanistic way of student learning. Cultural specificity should get embedded in the pedagogical practices which should be evolved for tribal, rural, urban communities and other ethnic groups.

A learning society visualises education as a continuing activity. This is equally applicable to teacher education. The policy stipulation on inseparability of the pre-service and in-service education of teachers and emphasis on continuing education need to be given pragmatic shape at the implementation stage. The curriculum of pre-service and in-service teacher education has to be redesigned to maintain continuity between the two. Teachers who are being educated today will have to devote major part of their life to education during the twentyfirst century. If the present rate of explosion of knowledge continues, in a few years the teachers will find themselves in a world where their present knowledge and teaching skills to an extent would become obsolete. They will have to face the challenge of electronic media and information technology.

One of the major inputs towards enhancing the quality of teaching and learning in schools as well as the teacher education institutions would be the extent to which research outputs and the outcomes of innovations are utilised by the system. Researches on teacher education have been and are being conducted in universities, national level institutions and other establishments but their utility for the teacher educator or the classroom teacher remains rather low.

Majority of the researches are undertaken to obtain a degree and hence the focus on its possible utility and relevance gets misplaced. The situation is compounded by non-availability of appropriate dissemination mechanisms, like journals, publication of findings in different forms and opportunities to the target group to get an access to these. Institutional capabilities and resources need to be augmented, enabling them to undertake relevant researches.

There is a definite requirement of bringing in research methods and methodologies in appropriate form in teacher education at pre-service and in-service programmes. To an extent, it finds a place in master level courses in education though in some universities the same is not insisted upon. The structure and design of future courses and programmes need to take this aspect into account. Preparation of teacher educators can no longer be completed without adequate grounding in various aspects of research. Researches must respond to policy issues, curriculum issues, evaluative procedures and practices, training strategies, classroom practices etc. The areas of teacher preparation for children with special needs, gifted children and children from groups with specific cultural, social and economic needs can no longer be ignored. Surveys and studies also need to be encouraged. These may be exploratory or diagnostic in nature. The new initiatives and innovations need to be encouraged and studied. Wherever considered appropriate, these could be brought into the system of teacher education for wider and gainful use.

2

TEACHING STRATEGIES

Commonly, the ideal of education is sought to be realised through teaching. In teaching, the teacher is the most important element if only because he has to annihilate himself, if only because he must appear to be the least important. This extremely delicate paradoxical part, teacher is called upon to play is seldom played well and the common failure to play it well dooms teaching to sterility. It is not enough if the teacher pays lip-homage to the principles a rigid adherence to which alone can avert failure. Everything depends upon the question whether the teacher puts the principles of true teaching into real living practice. These principles are described below:

Firstly, in teaching a subject, the teacher must look out and avoid the ever-tempting danger of teaching it in the ordinary sense of the word. It is easy for the teacher to teach a subject in this sense and fancy that it is teaching, and just because this is so, the danger of false teaching becomes more difficult to avoid. Most teachers are, therefore, found sooner or later on the wrong side. It is absolutely necessary to distinguish between false and true teaching. It may afford information and sometimes even interesting and valuable information possessing more than a passing life, but far from being education, it is exactly that which keeps the young from the path of true teaching. Educationists speak of the educative value of this, that and the other school-subject and teachers launch them on the classes stripped of all of this value. The result is inattention languor, futility or the fidgets and the numerous juvenile offences that are so common in schools and happily so rare in homes. The failure of any great ideal is fraught with dangers. The airman attempting the sky cannot afford to play with the balance of his craft. The failure of education which involves the whole field of young human life must make many young minds cruising the air in the early morning of existence crash.

Secondly, in teaching the pupils must work. This may seem too platitudinous and is in a way included in what has been said above. But the evil of made-easy education has gone so far that even a very platitude needs to be re-stated. True work implies volition, attention, perseverance and aim. True work is the mine from which right character is obtained. If education ought to form a wise preparation for life it must mean a well ordered system of work to receive its benefits.

Thirdly, in teaching it is not what the teacher does that matters so much as what he is. In fact there is nothing more vital to teaching than what the teacher is. He is the teacher for us who is a true testimony of teaching. The fortunes of teaching are staked on what he might be in one great pitch and toss. True teaching cannot fail. It is false systems wearing the mask of teaching that fail and have failed. It is the doubtful teacher that has failed. It is false instruction that lies defeated and exposed. Teaching is a sovereign remedy. It is the quack methods that are often practised in the name of teaching that fail us in the hour of great expectation. The need is urgent to clear educational ideals of false silt.

LAMPS OF TEACHING

To one that is born with a talent for the profession the greater lamps of teaching come unsought. They will have to seek them for long who are not thus born. However, every willing teacher can perhaps be a good teacher as well. If it is bad to stuff a child with food it is worse to stuff him with easy rudiments mere information or even with learning. The mechanism of physical well being will not long bear the strain of excessive food. Likewise the heaping of information on the child's mind must retard its growth and diminish its strength. He teaches trash who stuffs his pupils but it is a sad temptation and few really overcome it. Many do not know that there it is to battle. With a sepcies of enthusiasm that lends them an air of rightousness, they pile inert matter upon the tender minds because the idea has not simply occurred to them that it may not be quite the right thing to do. It is a cunning enemy that takes us captive without out knowledge.

Wisdom, love and work are the primary lamps of teaching. Their blended lights must illuminate education if it is ever to rise from the mechanical transformation which it has undergone in modern times.

Lamp of Wisdom

Wisdom is the first great lamp of teaching. It may seem at the first blush that if this is the thing we want it may be next to impossible to find it. The quantity of wisdom that lurks in the unfashioned immensity of the universe is ever so small. The wise among the race of men are but a mere handful and their services are needed elsewhere than in the classroom. It may, therefore, be feared that the profession of teaching may have to be content with something less than the illumination of wisdom's lamp. But although wisdom is like a needle in hay, everyone comes into the world with the instinct of wisdom. And if this instinct frequently languishes in the course of growth, we must quarrel with ourselves not with our Creator. It is the prime duty of the teacher to nourish this inborn instinct of His so that he might be able to show the way it might be nourished to those who come to sit at His feet.

Wisdom rises from the experiences of the physical and mental senses of man. Wisdom is the child of abundant life. It is not to be gained from the ordinary renunciations, from the ordinary inhibitions that we sometimes like to impose on ourselves. The narrow outlooks, the curious obsessions, the obstinate obliquities that we often come across at every turn spring from restricted experience from limited life.

The teacher whose job is to tell others the way to live must have a view of things embracing the whole of life in most of its aspects. He must have a sense of the diverse experiences that fall commonly to the lot of men. It is from such sense that wisdom rises. But the teacher is most commonly the one who has often the least of this sense.

He often lives as it were in a kind of backwater way from the living currents fed by the eternal and everyday forces of life. He does not usually know that abundance of life which comes from broad sympathies and wakeful impulses. He usually lives an exclusive life, and often cherishes in a manner of speaking a communalism of intellect which is not always intellectual. It must seem strange if one thinks about it that the work of preparing youngsters for life is entrusted to elders whose knowledge of it is often so restricted.

The lamp of wisdom without which teaching must largely remain dim may fill us with a certain gloom because it must seem to lie somewhat out of our reach. It is the inherent nature of good things to cover themselves with rough garbs. If the profession can convince itself of the use of this lamp it can get it also. There is not a school teacher who can live more fully, think more daringly and read more eagerly. There is not one who can aspire to a larger share of the great heritage of knowledge of that wondrous book of experience whose alphabets have been fashioned by time. There is really not one that does not keep alive in some hidden recess of his mind a desire for culture for wisdom and for that power of moving minds which culture and wisdom give. It is in fact for the lamp of wisdom that we are stretching out our hands; but if we would have it, we must go nearer it before we begin streching out our hands.

The teacher has need of the mild-hued light that falls from wisdom—the first great lamp of teaching. And he will not come by it unless he consents to become an ardent student of life and continually pushes forward the borders of his interests. He is the interpreter of the eternal ever changing panorama of life to the young and on his acceptation of the meanings of things largely depends their future. He must eschew nothing from his intellectual domain not even the controversies of politics, which some would from excessive solicitude. He must read and imbibe, observe and understand, meditate and grow wise. It is the passions that surround him and attain that calm strength which is no less useful in the class room than in the chambers of kings and of rulers of men.

In the eyes of society today the teacher may be an insignificant figure but he cannot get a larger space in it by simply asking for more. He must rise to his true dignity, reach his true stature first hold uprightly the great lamp of wisdom in his hand and then perhaps he will have little need to measure his proportions in the eyes of others. If he achieves the wisdom we have been contemplating if he seizes that shining lamp he will have acquired his place in the sun and in the great scheme of common things.

Lamp of Love

If the teacher has come by the lamp of wisdom he must also come by the lamp of love. Wisdom is the product of the reactions of our senses on the world of things. Love is the product of our humanity acting upon our wisdom. Wisdom lightens the subtle mystery of our inner nature. Where the light from the lamp of wisdom mingles with the gentel illumination of the lamp of love, there is born that understanding which holds the beginnings of all great things. Let these two lamps be kept burning on either side of teaching to keep reproaches away, to quench the futilities that now encumber education.

Love pre-supposes understanding. The teacher must get to know his pupils to love them. If he does not do this he cannot love them either in the only effective way. His love of his pupils can function that is in the way of making them better of helping them to see themselves. Every teacher of sorts usually indulges in the love jargon and practises some imitiation of love. Such love is often even worse than hatred. It only injures the ideal of education. It only helps to make the young slipshod which is about the greatest danger can overtake them.

There is nothing more easy than to insinuate injurious notions into the young in the early blush of promise. Adolescence and the years approaches it are tossed by many errant gales and we cannot trust maudling sentiment to steer young boys and girls safely through them. If love is apt to make the teacher weak instead of giving him additional strength and reinforced resolve it were best to keep that lamp unlighted. The weaker variety of love is fraught with danger to its object. A school treated with such love becomes a clamorous assembly of educational ineptitudes.

Lamp of Work

The third lamp without which the teacher can hardly attain his true stature is the lamp of work. There is a lurking danger in the teaching profession, and it is that it provides opportunities to those who like to avoid work without appearing to do so. It sometimes gives an air of virtue to what is not really different from vegetation. It sometimes covers private indolence with a look of disinterested public service.

Every great ideal which the high-souled among man kind has given us is, in some degree, hospitable to spirits that nurse a kind of secret animosity to it. Thus, in the teaching profession, which calls for the utmost powers of the toiling man, are often found individuals with a certain aversion to work, with a certain hankering after idle safety. This is perhaps more or less true of every co-operative effort touching society at large, but the teaching profession is, perhaps, in a special degree, kind to 'back-sliders' seeking the time of their lives.

Teachers must be workers in the highest sense, because the happy useful life, to which it is their duty to take the rising generations, is itself purely and completely a product of work. It is the worker who is happy and for whom the world has use. It is only the worker who can inspire the young with the spirit of work. Therefore, the teacher who shuns work is like an idle camp-follower hanging on the army of progress. He is not help but impediment. Then again work is the great purifier of life, the destroyer of passions, the bringer of inward peace. If the schools of today are not free from the jealousies and envies of low natures, it is because there are evading elements of idleness in them which stealthily rouse men to evil little hostilities. Each idle teacher must sooner or later shape into a 'sect' and look upon his brothers with suspicious eye. If a school contains some teachers of this type, it must be said to live in a calamity.

DISCIPLINE

Discipline comes from good education and good education is made better education by discipline. The position partakes of the nature of a riddle to some degree. It perhaps requires some elucidation. Right teaching is sound education, which means self-education much more than passive reception of what is told. The greater part of right teaching must consist in the teaching of pupils by themselves for themselves. Even class-teaching to be worth anything at all must be based on this principle. The teaching of pupils by themselves for themselves means occupation to the pupils, and rightly done, an occupation of absorbing interest. Occupation is orderliness, which is also called discipline is to be desired which is the one and only type of discipline worth having. The students must get to live in the idea that they come to school to learn. Secondly, when once they are gathered in the school they must be given the opportunity to work and learn.

The astonishingly large amount of idleness that one meets within the average schools of today is a great menace to education. Idleness, which is about the same thing as emptiness has never been known to be kind to education. On the other hand all work is education of a sort. Mere unoccupied idleness, the hundred per cent inactivity, is not to be expected from boys whose minds and limbs are restless, impatient to grasp and see and understand thousand new things that meet them in a new world of numberless surprises and shocks. If, therefore, the school refuses them work they will do their best they can to find it for themselves. It may be first the school rules that they choose to lay hands on. Or it may as well be their teachers themselves, whom they generally so much like to study by provoking some fermentation in their behaviour. Idleness puts on the physiognomy of useless and hurtful activity in one or another of its manifold forms. Beckoning chances in pleasing postures line the road from mere inattention in the classroom to sex experience. It must be owned that these too have some education to give but the trouble is that it is not to receive this education that young boys and girls come to schools.

Indiscipline in the sense we have understood is very much in evidence today in most educational institutions. One of the commonest cause of this indiscipline is the failure of class teaching as it has been practised. If any one thinks that listening is an easy enough art he does not probably know what he is thinking. In that form of class teaching which has almost universally established its dominance in education the teachers work the pupils witness, the teachers speak the pupils hear. It is not so much as listening as merely hearing. Listening entails some conscious controlled activity of mind. Such activity is too much to expect from the very young.

Grown-up people having some experience of the amenities of the platform need not be told how soon they tire to even real eloquence, how soon boredom creeps into them. That is why successful eloquence is so rare. It is sheer senselessnes if not inhumanity unintended though to ask the young a hungering for exploration in a world just unfolding its mysteries to them to sit in correct docility and listening passively to the words of reputed wisdom that fall from the teachers' lips like so many magic statues. Even words of the highest beauty and wisdom throbbing with the fire of life and the power to rule do not always get the atmosphere they deserve. And therefore when teaching takes the shape of telling unless it be amply aided by force and unless the teacher is endowed with the rarest gifts indiscipline must steal in with crafty cheerfulness which is its normal gesture. It is a good sign after all. It means that boys and girls tender as they are cannot easily be subjugated. It means that they bear in their bosoms enough health to stand out a siege or two. Although surrender might be quite welcome to the school authorities it must be reckoned a loss if the sum of possible human values not monentary gains is what matters in education no less than in progress.

When people talk about indiscipline they do so with an unconscious certainly that the school rules and school methods of teaching are the last word in this line. They would put down breaches with a heavy hand. They would shut the mouth that talks, simply run a hole in the ear that is closed and crunch the fingers that scribe on the wall. It is all delightfully funny and what is more than that it is sometimes effective too. Only it is absolutely wrong. Given the proper opportunity for work the question of discipline need never rise for all we know. But suppose this opportunity is not there try as we might for all we are worth, indiscipline must continue to speak in various little acts that arise from the irrepressible impulses of the young.

TEACHERS AND GENERAL KNOWLEDGE

The more the teacher knows the better he teaches. It is true that his main function is not to impart knowledge but he has to import some knowledge and what is more than that to impart it well. Now, to impart knowledge in a good way the person who seeks to impart it must have much more than he proposes to give. What comes from a well stocked mind bear a simplicity and sweetness which we do not find in what comes from a poorly endowed one. The person who knows little teaches much and pompously and also, ineffectively but he that knows much generally teaches little and quietly and also fruitfully. It is in educational institutions more perhaps, than anywhere else that empty vessels make the loudest sound.

The teacher is apt to be misled by the apparent smallness of the volume of knowledge that he is required to impart to his pupils into the belief that much knowledge is useless to him. The number of teachers who are thus misled is, perhaps, not small. One very often comes across the charge that teachers are as a class averse from reading and constantly replenishing their minds. It is not altogether a groundless charge but the reasons given for the aversion are often groundless.

The only reason applicable to the majority of cases is that teachers are unable to see what benefits could possibly result from as siduously refurbishing themselves. Most men are practical especially most ordinary men and they will not long give their time and energies to the pursuit of things whose value in terms of the immediate needs of life appears to them quite uncertain if not decidedly negligible.

All teachers desire freedom of work and payment adequate to their needs. The complaint is common that the teacher is often led by the nose if not a dog's life by those who are placed above him such as the Headmaster or the Inspector. The average teacher does not always feel quite like himself in the school world. He is frequently a captive, a victim, a trodden aspiration in it. He must evidently increase his power if he wants to be anything better and knowledge certainly must prove power to him. Increased knowledge would yield him a greater sense of confidence if not immediately in the long run, inspire a greater regard for him in his superiors, a greater faith in him in his pupils. Through knowledge he can attain that mental emancipation which is the only remedy within the reach of all the excessive outside control.

The teacher whose knowledge is not adequate cannot fully know the joy of teaching. The teacher, who has only a half penny worth in the way of knowledge, is bound to be a drudge, a melancholy mechanic unable to give himself or his class any joy. He is a cheerless driver of routine, a lifeless spoke in a rolling wheel. Knowledge will make him young and alive. And the gathering of knowledge is itself a real joy or at least becomes a joy after a time. A sense of knowledge brings with it a sense of elevation of exaltation a power that makes for us to hold up our heads.

USE OF QUESTION METHOD IN TEACHING

The question method is best and its exaltation were it to spring from actual practice, wisest. There is a running streak of disobedience in the mental inheritance of man. There is an instinct in it that faces order with impassivity that turns a deaf ear to both advice and exhortation. The young as well as the old often resist to be edified but are willing and often eager to discover. From the pulpit come flowing waves of somnolence. The telling teacher whatever be the content of his words, sooner or later breathes the soporific air. It is the immemorial way of letting sleeping dogs lie. But so soon as one begins to ask a question the eyes open and the mind awakens with a start. It is true that the mind does not always like to be thus rudely disturbed and no doubt it is sweeter to bang the eye lids than to keep them alert ever. No enemy is thanked when he threatens the tranquility of the throne. But the question is a challenge and the pupil feels that it must be tackled to preserve his pride. It threatens him into grity and he fights it. One cannot sleep with a question under his pillow or have peace when it probes his mind.

The question method must rule the roast wherever education is truthfully rendered. It may be easier for the teacher to spout information than to fusillade the class. And the bulk of students would be willing to pay him the heavy tribute of silent docility rather than sit under a running fire. The armoured teacher is therefore a hated figure in schools and the meek and gentle preacher softly telling the beads of learning is lifted to affectionate eminence.

There is no doubt that a habit of smiling and telling is no small asset to the teacher but not asset, however great can perhaps compensate the suspension of the question putting habit. There is no doubt that the larger the space allotted to questions in the classroom the richer the quality of the instruction. One may chalk out and tell over and over again the same things to be only forgotten when the voice pauses or the duster sweeps the board, but ask a question and it stings the mind, makes mouths at it, as it were compelling it to enter the lists.

The victories of the educational war are not easily matched by those of the educational peace. It is too late in the day to doubt the wisdom of Socrates. A courteous sense of gratitude has lifted the first putter of questions above question. And we are all agreed that "The mind to be kept in health must be kept in exercise."

One often comes across classes that are impervious even to questions. It is a sign of the chronic slumber arising from one or another educational luxury. They have been perhaps fed too much on digested information or left too long to sleep. They have been perhaps told things so long and so often that they have been left too little to themselves to desire understanding. When questions fail to stir a class, it is time to ask what it is suffering from. There is obviously some derangement in the mechanism of its impulses. The essential character of right questioning is such that even a fool might ask a question to witness the sight of ten wise men madly awaking to answer it.

Questions may be divided into three classes: questions to test memory; to test knowledge; to stimulate thinking. The first are the easiest to ask and the easiest to answer. Even these are fromidable enough in the placid and docile atmosphere of some classrooms. It may however be stated that there is perhaps no teacher or pupil that entirely escapes their association and in these examination ridden days they have in fact become the handmaiden of coaching. A question is asked and the bolts of memory loosen to the key. When mere memory questions gain the upperhand in classroom practice the question-method naturally suffers disesteem for the chief purpose of classroom questions is to spur the pupils to sit and think.

A distinction has been drawn between questions testing memory and questions testing knowledge. Perhaps it required explanation. Memory is an ill-assorted store. Things taken from the external world are often simply stowed away in it like so much disused material taking up room. This is what is called cram in the colloquial language of schools which is sometimes of such moment at examinations. Memory questions concern themselves about these little hoards of alien matter in the mind. Knowledge is different. It is the product of the action of the external world of objects and experience on the internal world of intellect. The cognition is accompanied by a chemical change. Things are not simply taken but altered, and altered, they are absorbed in the personality of the individual. This product that enters personality and enriches it by becoming one with it is knowledge and is often somewhat inaccurately called culture and question to test this intellectual element and assist its further development are of the highest value. "Who were the contending parties in the World War?" is a memory question. "Mention one of the chief causes that led to this war and explain it," is a knowledge-question. It calls for some insight and skill on the part of the teacher to stimulate and build up knowledge by questions and it will tax the pupils to the straining point to meet them bravely. The real question methods is not anywhere not certainly in any book for the teacher of children to have for the gathering.

Questions to test and stimulate thinking are by far the most significant function of the question and answer method of teaching. In parliaments and popular councils the question time often given governments furiously to think. The putter of searching questions draws down on his head the esteemed ordium of the powers that be. Early man learned to rise by asking questions of the external phenomena. Science builds its glittering towards on the living rocks of the question-method. The great thinkers have always ascended to glory or doom the twin-born awards to higher earthly existence. And teaching to think is of such vast importance that it is necessary to speak of it in single place.

TEACHING TO THINK

To think is to live for thought is the soul of things. The boundary between life and non-life is fading away. The heart-throbs of the inanimate atom are little less wonderful than the highest flights of man's imagination. The Universe is sprung of thought. Whether the idea was born in God for immanence does not matter so long as the symmetry of the Universe, the harmony of the spheres compels the conception of some great imperative imagination as having been the cause of it all. Neither does it matter if there is or no thought in the living and non-living materials that surround us. For creation is thought and the rolling words in pathless space must lose their ways were it not for some over-seeing wisdom standing by and bidding them bear themselves along the destined courses.

In keeping in mind the importance of thought stimulation in the educative process the teacher perhaps needs to be forewarned against certain spurious forms of thought which are peculiarly fertile source of deception in modern times. More people in these days think themselves thinkers. The claim can hardly be maintained. It is true that the pretence deceive themselves as much as it does others but that does not make the danger of counterfeit thought any the less. In the age when the daily output of ideas from the press almost hourly get increased in volume and more and more insistent and the bread winning business of ordinary folks tends to put more and more strain on their none too plentiful energies it is only natural that thinking is readily borrowed, sometimes unconsciously and afterwards as readily mistaken for one's own ware. It is, therefore commonly seen that most people especially the literate classes are inclined to pose as thinkers while in reality they are only borrowers of thought.

The classroom is not immune from this danger for boys and girls are not averse from learning the tricks and manners of their elders. The teacher has certainly to distinguish between thinking and thinking to be able to tell the authentic metal however unpolished it is presented from the uttered currency however genuine the latter might appear. The first sincere efforts of the juvenile mind do not easily take polish. On the other hand, their rough style can tell the teacher that his peoples are on the right track.

The teacher perhaps will have himself to think to be able to teach thinking. He himself will have to provide the real article to evoke it in his pupils to tempt them to the skies and lead the way. This is perhaps a tall order. However, more than the silent teacher makes the silent class the thinking teacher makes the thinking class and the best way for the teacher to learn thinking if he happens to have not learnt it is to begin thinking, striving to give his own responses to the appeal of the objects and experiences about him.

Is it not a common practice to bewail the monotony of teaching? While the succeeding batches of peoples come up against succeeding layers of new things the teacher is regretted for his being obliged to stay put in the same layer. He is not always aware that he may have himself to thank. Whatever be the subject he teaches he can switch it into new light every time he teaches it if he is sufficiently awake to its possibilities and in the measure he teaches it freshly he must stir the minds of his pupils.

The teacher has therefore to be a thinker for his own sake and if he is that he gradually extends the thoughtful care to his pupils. It is fatal for the teacher to clap the extinguisher on his mind and to remain immured within the four corners of his bald routine. There is no more distressing sight than the old and experienced teacher lading out instruction from his frowsy granery of notes. The thing is a curious fulfilment of the school curriculum although according to the strick letter of the law it might be just the right and proper thing to do.

Another important thing to be remembered is that excessive information is the enemy of thought. Too much fuel congests the fire. It is better to tend it than to press it with wood if the intention is to make it burn brighter and brighter. To swathe the pupils in adipose information is certainly more easy than to be the vestal guardians of the minds. Mental food is slow to digest and if undigested clogs the wheels of the mind more than undigested physical food does the organs of the body. The motto of mental purveyor ought to be, to give little by little slowly and slowly. It is neither possible nor even advisable to force the pace of the young mind.

Some of the directions in which the teacher of thinking likely to receive help may now be briefly considered. There is indeed no subject which gives a chance to the teacher to awake thought in his pupils. Even history does which seems to the days completely domesticated to the purposes of cram. Do the pupils realise that in history they are offered opportunities of holding converse with their own ancestors? Are they in any way affected by the pageant of civilisations rising, flourishing and sinking to doom?

History is pre-eminently a subject to call for and educate the feelings and the human imaginations which is an intimate part of the mechanism of thinking. It is difficult to exaggerate the importance of nourishing and educating the feelings, for man is ninety per cent feeling and ten percent other things. They are the engine of action and no wise education endeavour can spare any effort to make them strong and to make them wise. History invites such effort but more than otherwise the soul of history is forgotten. All this is a fresh reminder that unless the teacher is willing to help education cannot get much chance to become progressively satisfying to the need of life.

TEACHING BY STORY-TELLING

No good teacher either of the young or of the adult ever discarded the services of the story. No prophet striving to be honoured in his own country was above their aid. The Buddha, Jesus and Mohammed treated their inspired wisdoms with similes and parables before they offered them to their countrymen. The mother and the child sail the seas of fancy and dream like Wynken, Blynken and

Nod on Fable's flying craft. The preacher adorns his ethics with an ancient tale. The speaker strives to uplift the falling eyelids without losing heart until he has improvised the story of a man that burned down his house to secure relief from its alien population of rats. Incipient Rome averted a division by the stratagem of a single story in which the silent stomach vindicated its selfishness.

The old schoolmaster mitigated his stick with an occasional dose of story. The fool in the play finds his daily bread in saucy yarn. The lingering grandmother assuages her age and embellishes the home by putting on a general show of green memories. The forgotten old man sets up as a raconteur and recovers his lost place in the sun.

Should an Englishman come to a remote Indian village and tell the children a story they listen to him never minding the little inconvenience interposed by their total ignorance of the English language. It is perhaps not a mere story that stories were one of the chief causes of the emergence of man from his first savage condition. The teacher of the present day need not be ashamed if he should happen to tell a story or even more than one story to his yearning young *chelas*.

In the hands of discerning teacher, on the other hand, the story wisely chosen and well told is a powerful weapon of education. It gives the sugar-coating to unamiable knowledge, the window dressing or the market touch which is also the human touch to morality, the frosty shoulder to fatigue or languor, the hospitable hearth to interest and to those intimate personal relations between teacher and pupil without which the humanity of the teacher cannot come under full play in the expansion and elevation of the class. A story artistically rendered braces up the teacher even sooner than it does the class. It is twice blessed in a more immediate sense than mercy directly blessing him that gives and him that takes. And because it is twice blessed its employment often tends to become too frequent by those who have enjoyed its graces. Appetite grows with eating and all story and no stern instruction is apt to make the pupils soft and even dull.

The elements that help to make the teacher a story-teller are a gift of narration, a sense of sympathy and humour, a measure of imagination, a ready power of analysis of swift and brief assembling of incidents and of leading the divisions with a skilful disposition of emphasis and harmony. The difference between reading a story and telling it is the difference between building a house and buying one. You build a house after your own heart. You buy one to cajole yourself into appreciation of certain architectural ideas which you probably do not share and even if you should you cannot instinctively applaud for the simple reason that you have had no hand in their expression. The teller of the story must live a story to tell it well. He must give the gestures of his mind to it the flavour of his personality something of the savour of his own fancies to it so that the story might be given not merely a rehearsal but life. It is essential that although the story is borrowed feathers he must not hesitate to shine in them.

In telling a story the teacher can remember certain 'rules' to advantage. The narration must be slow; swift and natural. The substance must increase at a quicker pace than the telling. The telling must also be natural so that as the narrative is uncovered it might lose its character as a story to become an experience. The dramatic element is part and parcel of the story-telling art. It does not mean that the teller has got to away and dance and press into service all the mad gestures of which he is incapable. The dramatic element is not often theatrical. The 'play' often brings down the house with the least 'acting' heaving on the boards. The soul of the drama is contained in its emotional quality. Its success is conditioned by the amount of delicate representation of this quality the actor is able to save from his activities. And the hidden art being the best art, the expression of the feelings must be subtle, elusive and unsubstantial. It is, therefore, highly important that the teller not only enters into the spirit of the story and loses himself in it but also remembers himself all the time, in which case he will not easily tip himself over the edge of the dramatic element into melodrama. It is for the hearers to be flamboyant in their feelings, for they can do no harm.

The right stories, sombre or bright are essentially entertainment but are not without use great use one must say simply because they are essentially entertainment. Far from being useless stories are the most helpful of things in the education of the emotions. Stories are mostly men and women even when they are birds and beasts as they are and were as they could be if they would as they should be if they would strive enough as they ought to be by whatsoever means.

Stories are humanity in the lump, men and women of all ranks, of all times, of all ages. They are the unofficial history of human beings and therefore their human value is much greater than histories of nations and countries. In the infinite variety of life and its changing problems they are the one eternal common factor. They speak of one and all in language understanded of one and all. They fascinate the lowest savages and inform the most superior men. They delight the children and brighten the extreme old. They read lessons to all. They persuade men and women to love men and women, to help and be happy while they may. They are human nature elevating human nature telling the feelings to be good, the passions to behave, the desires to be wise, the aspirations to be true and the ideals to be beautiful.

LESSON PREPARATION

Preparation is not only the beginning of teaching but also a considerable part if not the first half of it. Conscientious preparation is of the best as well as of the highest aspect of the teacher's work. If one knows a subject thoroughly one needs must speak or write about it or teach it. One cannot hide one's light under a bushel when it is really bright. Self-expression is a psychological need and if the mind is full, self-expression becomes a necessity.

Teaching whatever it may not be is self-expression which when it springs from an honest mental urge is generally so warm and shining that there is rare self-satisfaction no less than rare influence. It is, therefore, difficult to exaggerate the importance of preparing a lesson before it is actually uncovered in the class. This might at the first blush seem a pretty stiff thing to say but as teaching is an easy and at the same time an excellent means of self-expression the teacher might prepare a lesson to teach and grind as axe of his own into the bargain.

If a lesson should be what it ought to be a thing that informs the head and feeds the heart it must be fresh, spontaneous, real and sincere. These qualities are the same that give distinction to every variety of effort, that give art its timeless appeal, that inspire the hard and humble labours with shy and simple litanies of joy. Work is exalted because no work whatever be its nature is unfit or incapable of attaining these qualities and work is also hated because the worker not minding them enough often misses them in his work. These castles is the air might not seem to be connected with the bourgeois business of classroom practice if preparation is denied, its counsel in the sum of its quality. It however needs little reflection to see that even to teach what one knows well one must know better so that one may teach it best, which is almost the same thing as saying that even to teach what one knows best one must know a little better than best so that one may teach it well.

No preparation is apparently necessary to teach a young class what it means. And yet if the teacher thinks about it before hand he is likely to see that it can open some new prospects. The rhyme is a little one's dream, a dream of coming joy. He is a born tiller of land. He is already tilling in fancy and feeling the quivering seed in his hand. He sees with the zest of a prophet of soil the agriculture grow and the harvest ripen. His imagination is strong and he reaps the harvest and binds the sheaves and carries the shocks home. Meanwhile, the grass is grown tall and he mows it and makes it into hay when the sun shines, and look how he pitches it up on the rick when he is a man! The little boy is playing the farmer better than many farmers plough and sow and reap the corn and pile up the hay. There is the tingle of ecstasy in the dream. It is utterly sincere. The rural sense has him and he dances to its voice. There never was a more enchanted gospel of the land.

In an agricultural country such as India, the little boy's dreaming joy can easily assume a practical fervour and the opportunity of reading education in terms of life comes to the teacher. The agricultural children of whom there must be a considerable number of almost all Indian schools will thank the teacher for a chance to become vocal and autobiographical. "Have you ever ploughed the ground?" "How is the seed sown?" "What is a rick?" "How is the rick made?" "Have you ever raked hay?" such inquiries must coax the children to empty their confidences self-obliviously and the hour is overflown with the piping voices, and should the teacher also have a contribution of his own to fare forth with the poem imperceptibly becomes a festival of fond memories. All which goes to show that one cannot know any thing too well to look at it carefully for a space before he takes it to the class.

It is true that the best lesson is that which grows in the class. Transplantation is the enemy of spontaneity. But every creation is twice-born. The play is written before the footlamps are lighted. The house is drawn before brick and mortar are called. The lesson is prepared before it is taught. It cannot grow in the class from a void. As the plant grows from soil the lesson grows from a congenial collection of apperceptions and the more congenial the apperceptions are the more spontaneous natural and vivid the lesson rises. The class may be said to be a small and intense kingdom of big and unexpected surprises and the teacher cannot be too resourceful to manage its affairs. If he be not a ready teacher, he can hardly be a ready anything else while the needs of the kingdom require him continually to be ready to do so many things. The secret of ready teaching is preparation and the weakest link in the chain of preparation is the measure of the teacher's strength.

The presentation of the lesson, whenever it is good is a mingling of more than one line of procedure. Roughly these lines of procedure are the grammatical and logical and the psychological. Grammar is concerned with modes of expression. It may be said to be the etiquette of things. Grammatical teaching has its value but it is apt to take an ell where only an inch is due or given. The grammatical view of life, once it gets a foothold, generally touches the atmosphere pretty heavily with its superficial and obtrusively symmetrical solemnities and it is easier to render education grammatical than even to teach so called grammar strictly. The logical procedure is more logical than the grammatical although both are concerned more or less with externalities. Abstract reasoning, which is logic is a much too equivocal and unpractical a drug to be administered to the young. The High School need not be too consciously averse from the matter of reasoning processes but should attempt in vain to impress the higher pleasure of pure reason on its juvenile population. The psychological method is by far better than either the grammatical or the logical for adoption at least in the lower forms in the High School, in other words, there had best be a heavier ingredient of psychology than of logic or grammar in school lessons.

It is therefore, necessary to say what is here meant by the psychological method. The science of the mind is the seeker of the meaning of things. It tackles the life tissues and although these often lie deep they are not out of the reach of even the youngest understanding. The function of education is to give life, more life and still more life and the teacher must pour life forth to the children, good measure, pressed down and shaken together and running over and then he shall have himself overflowing abundance. It is the meaning of plants and animals of elements and atoms of the call of the mountain and of the sea of river and city of picture and song that the teacher is there to interpret. In the true lesson the trappings and shows fade beyond the margin of the day.

There is all the difference between preparing a lesson and writing correct notes of lessons. Obedience to the rule and evasion of the substance is a hoary human habit, and the rule is often stiffened to the greater evasion of the substance. Neither the rule nor the evasion is worth the candle. The true lesson is above 'notes of lessons' because it is prepared and it is prepared because it is the only way to teach it well and teach it with pleasure.

In the preparation and presentation of a lesson it is possible to be exactingly analytical. Analysis, though unexceptionable is liable to be overdone. To split gossamer is as futile as to paint the lily and as bad. To think to tell a pea from a pea is to miss the mystery of peas. Whatever the subject a too generous use of needle and knife ends as the enemy of self-expression on the part of the pupils. The possibility of teaching a subject excessively will have, therefore, be borne in mind in the preparation of lessons. The purpose of explanations is to quicken thought and wonder. They must pause directly the purpose is gained; otherwise the mind instead of the explanations pauses. This is the educational 'checkmate' arising from the examination instruction so widely practised in these days.

Intensive teaching rigorously pursued often cribs the mind. It fills the mind by taking from it its hunger and appetite. Digressive teaching on the other hand opens out new vistas expanding the mind. It feeds the mind by increasing its bunger and appetite. The open air is always better than the bedizened antechamber. Ventilation is the water of life in teaching. The anecdote armed the parable hearing the story laden wanderer has often a truer sense of teaching than the methodical instructor steeped up to the eyes in the grammar and dictionary and discipline of the lesson in hand. For the class lesson is not a museum piece but a life-process a free excursion rather than a dull and enforced encampment. The preparation will therefore involve other things than the lesson itself and the larger the number of these other things the richer the subsequent teaching.

CHARACTER BUILDING

Character is such a frequently used word that its connotation is diffused in the common speech of the day. Almost everybody has something to say about it and often something sensible and helpful. Yet our ideas about character are none too clarified. Character is too complex a human expression for analysis to reveal fully its ravelled skein. Our knowledge of character is however, sufficient to help us to realise its importance and to approach it with the hushed spirit of inquiry it deserves. Character is a question of human worth, the determining factor in man. It is the compound of all of the man's action and thought. It is the cast of his self's countenance which is above his powers of display or disguise. More than the face is the index of the mind, character is the index of the whole of him. Character is at once the summary and sum total of the man.

Although it is not known for certain it is generally believed that we are born with our characters partly made and that we make it fuller and fuller as we grow. Heredity is often said to be a more powerful influence in human life than it is generally supposed and the hereditary elements in character are often described to be far from negligible. There is no doubt that we come into the world with mental and bodily tendencies. The old belief in the attendance of fairies at the `arrival' of children to give them legacies, good or bad, is a picturesque explanation of a more or less fundamental fact in human life by an impressive fable. Our fathers have remembered us in their wills but every inheritance has its price and their sins in varying degrees might have been visited upon us.

These considerations incite irresponsibility on the one hand and induce a measure of helplessness on the other. We are often persuaded to put on the abandoned supremacy of leaves blown in a storm and since it cannot be helped be regard life with lordly indifference. This attitude is however without justification in experience. Our native helplessness is immeasurable only because it is unmeasurable. The history of human endeavour is a blended archive of triumph and failure and the volume of failure is not bigger than that of victory. Perhaps it is much less. Progress is the testimony of man's power to shape his destiny. Science speaks his opportunities. Philosophy shows the pilgrimages open to him. Individuals prove their fitness to bear the brunt of battle and to brave the blows of circumstance. Look wherever we may from the raging of blind elements perhaps issuing from the dim regions that stretch behind our births from the wrecks of failure, from the jaws of defeat, man standing on the whole undefeated and undismayed, is able to bear fresh laurels home. It needs no psychology to come and tell us that although we are born each with his fate on his head the inevitable bundles can contain without themselves the alchemy for changing themselves. We live in an age of universal synthesis of transmutations of magic metals. The uprising of gold from mercury shows man's power to change the character of things. Man too, in a sense can and does change himself.

Democratic education not only consider all classes of people but also all conditions of intelligence. The feeble-minded have as much right to and as much expectation of finding themselves as the quick-witted. The Voltairian disbelief in the immutability of human inequalities can be now said to be bearing fruit. We are trying to explore the origins of personality to understand how best we might adapt them to the call of common and individual welfare. The results of this endeavour have however here and there, tinged the temper of modern educational movements with a certain amount of gloom.

Students of heredity and child-mind have in recent years greatly increased our wondering respect for children but this new child-sense is often found to contain elements of anxiety to escape the blame of mishandling them and of uneasy doubts if it is quite within our power to help them and to change them for the better. Psychological educationalists are often inclined to exalt the native side of character to something like primacy and to suspect the teacher's efforts to engender and build up the right tendencies and impulses in his pupils. This scientific recrudescence of armoured fate is an equivocal force in the educational field. It is possible to understand children too well. Free inquiry if pushed too far sometimes comes full circle and results in new obscurantism. Whatever fears and doubts psychology in its excavations into the infant human mind throws up teachers have to go forward without gratuitous qualms discovering the young for themselves. Voltaire is still good for them.

Character is invested with a double sovereignty. Its counsel is supreme in the iconography of individuals no less than in that of social values. Character fixes the individual's place in society no less than it fixes the individual himself. The function of the school is to bring these two apparently ill adjusted half parts of character into proper correlation. The innate and often explosive energy of selfishness has to be subdued by soft degrees to the ennobling appetite for service. The ill conducted passions swaying the individual mind have to be sublimated into a fairy jewelry of self-oblivious ideals.

The ultimate aim of education is to discover the individual for himself in society to adjust difference with uniformity without detracting much from either to make every individual a pride unto himself and at the same time a pillar of society. Unity and individuality in harmony are the goal. Anger can become an ally of soul-force greed, a golden hunger, lust a warm infusion of love and hatred an imperative impatience with evil. Society must value the individual and the individual must suffer society and serve it as well. Education cannot plead inability to see the wood for the trees or the trees for the wood. The ultimate test in both aspects is character.

Apart from the teacher and his personality which are certainly supreme among the factors that help the enterprise of founding character the school itself taken as a whole and functioning collectively may suggest signposts of thought and action to its juvenile inhabitants. A school without a tradition is nearly like the play of Hamlet without the prince. Traditions are active elements influencing character. The atmosphere is an invisible agent of change in body and mind.

The presence of a great man is an inspiration to the small more often than it is an envy. The Headmaster of a school has therefore got to have a personality of his own and a compelling sense of wholesale identification with the institution to build for the school a body of traditions so that the pupils through their silent influence may become better and better if necessary in spite of themselves and even without their knowledge. The school must have a stamp to impress upon its children but this does not mean making them the same but to making them strong each with himself and loyal each to his inner voices.

If the school is well supplied with sincerity and love, with discipline and freedom, with hungry satisfaction, with omnivorous zeal, with visible lineaments of courage and nobility, great pictures and haunting dreams it would be possible to wish it prosperity in its call to handle character. The school house may be simple but the class room must be inspiring. The teacher must naturally always remain the source of inspiration, the dominant actor in the play but the footlights and scenes help. The class room is a laboratory of character and the class rooms mingling their mild forces make the tradition of the school which the Headmaster sitting apart from indistinguishable from its assembled life fosters and guards with jealous care. The tradition of the school thus becomes the guarantee of its standards.

Nor should Nature be neglected. Green is good for the eyes. Woods and pastures blow bracing air on the mind. Gardens beckon thought and dream and lend them beauty. There is rich mental festival in pageants of plants and the children can by themselves make these pageants. If they do they should become beautiful which is it so very bad a thing to do? Nature the mother of all flowers helps character bloom. Let every school bear this in mind for there is need.

The curriculum of the school may as easily be made a cordon to keep away the sins as a mere manger for examination going folks. It is possible to make it a sort of classroom scouting an indoor exercise of the intellectual emotional and aesthetic elements that combine to produce character. Poetry, for instance is the sum of life and the most elegant guide to the feelings. To be able to appreciate poetry is to impart a soft and soaring culture into the mind that cannot fail to leaven the whole life.

Teaching poetry leaving appreciation unasked is much the same as teaching Nature without so much as requiring the students to look at her once. The appreciation may be little or great but when it totally fails the Mue gives the class the slip if more in shame than in annoyance. Poetry is the greatest school subject to give just the desired tonality to the primary chords of character.

The value of the school derives from the aspirations dreams and devotions it offers and not from the bulky avoirdupois of instruction it daily releases. This is an ancient fact which is consigned to oblivion for the amiable reason that it has been known to everybody; but the teacher who forgets it salving his qualms with the superior meditation that it is common and old gives capital short weight.

Poetry with its overwhelming joy and sorrow, beauty and truth, adventure, hallucination and vision is the food of the gods for the little beasts clamouring at the school gateway for their characters which they think not quite wrongly have been somewhat unlawfully detained in its inner recesses.

Imagination on the teacher's part should indeed enable him to bend every school subject to the purpose of building character. In a sense all that comes to his mind could be grist. History will give him human characters to emulate or fly from. Geography will uncover to him the characters of human beings in combination. Mathematics will come to him holding out the lure of abstracted intellect, of its service in the solution of human problems and of this unimpassioned influences like oil on troubled waters upon the passionate cauldron which it so very often is of the human mind. Science will tell him the supremacy of natural laws over all things including man and of the glory of understanding obedience to them. The school curriculum even when inadequate in quality or excessive in contents, can to some extent be made to give embodiment to the principles that underline conduct. If this is not generally done or perfunctorily done it is perhaps because it is easier to explain a subject than to ask it to stir the heart or to make it speak without the aid of an interpreter to the mind. There are sermons in stones and it is wonderful how instructive these could be incurably dumb as they are.

The playground is more senses than is common to suppose it is both a rearing place and a trial house of character. There is the most intimate contact between player and player. The individual is all important while the team is the ultimate factor. Competition waxes furious but actual conflict would be fatal to the common interest. There are the overseeing rules and everyone must play the game. It would be deemed a victory to strive nobly and to suffer defeat if that be the result cheerfully, as it would be deemed ignominious to spy out a chance to pinch a winking rule or to steal a march. The game is thus a faithful representation of the industrious honourable and mutually helpful and beneficial life that we meet with although none too frequently in a well ordered society that knows its job and therefore affords excellent apprenticeship to the citizens of tomorrow. Games obviously develop the body and stimulate its functions but this is not their chief pride, which they would rather keep secret. They develop character and prove it more they create it and endow it. A school without games is something like a public meeting summoned at the fag end of day without even the attraction of the presence of a single good speaker.

Do punishments help in building character? The question is more readily posed than answered. A wise writer has said that many things could be borne when the intention is good. The well intentioned Headmaster that applies the birch to an erring boy is often like captive good captain. Prison reform is proof of the failure of prisons. More hanging is frequently followed by more capital crime and when hanging is abolished capital crime is not unoften ashamed to rear its head.

Punishment is sometimes provocative of the very offences it would put down and if punishment is vindictive or is meted out as a warning it, having not even the excuse of good intension is extremely apt to be an incitement to more misdoing. Tyrants have always tried terrorism and have always failed. It all means only this that mankind is brave and still cherishes in its bosom the sin of its original unsubmissiveness and that men and women could be made to do or not to do many things which they would or would not do under the minatory forefinger of fear. The school must be the last place for corporal punishment to be practised in or rather the first place for it to be tried to be thrown away the next moment for good. Many a wild colt has turned out a noble steed in understanding sympathy. In kindly severity apart from physical punishment many that come to scoff remain to pray. On the other hand, how often a bad enough boy becomes worse and worse in the hands of teacher none of whom can get to like him probably because they would not seek to know him and how often the same boy the instant he is convinced that one teacher likes him becomes all right and one better to him. It is high time one is tempted to say that the birch was withdrawn from the hands of the educational profession for when punishment goes wrong and ninety nine out of one hundred times it is inflicted it is more than likely to go wrong it becomes to say the least of it a menace to character.

After all for the school to redeem its promises it must be a society. It must be a society every time it calls itself a school or answers to that name if it is to exert any tangible and beneficial influence on the juvenile springs of character. And the importance of the school lies in the fact that it can be made a model society not only for its own purposes but also for the immediate benefit of the neighbourhood.

The school cannot only be a preparation for the life but life itself at least in a measure as it should be. Every class can be a unit of self-rule with its own cabinet and code of laws and sanctions for breaches. Every class can contain the just juxtaposition of collective responsibility and individual vigilance. Every class can be its own parliament in which every citizen enjoys his right of say full democracy not the representative democracy of today which is often only symbolic self rule.

The larger school with its thronging numbers will be content with representative Swaraj but with nothing less than the best and most compact representative Swaraj. Unless the school thus blends life with learning character cannot come and the young individuals cannot see where their true natures lie, nay even learning must slowly vanish like a worn down stock of words. The atmosphere may thus become the breeding ground of many evils. The indefatigable energies of the young being denied the best channels of expression they must capture for themselves any means of expression which are often terrifying, both in their novelty and bravery. While their over wise elders engage themselves in not but generally barren discussions whether character could be made or amended or whether the children should be taught the mechanism of the genital organs or the etiology of too early sex, the sapient little ones, themselves tumultuously and emotionally rendezvoused in another place give exhibitions of their holy incorrigibility regaling one the other with their auticipations of sexual bliss.

DANGERS OF GOOD TEACHING

There are little dangers in the profession that rise out of the ground, as it were, to get hold of the teacher. It will take some vigilance, even a degree of luck, to give these dangers the slip. But if one is not able to escape them, whatever be one's worth, one loses that power of personality which, above all other things, in the teaching profession keeps the teacher's work from going barren. Some of these lesser dangers with regard to which the teacher has always to be 'on the Qui vive' are anger, intolerance, partiality, the popularity mania, rivalry and discontent.

The present is so real and insistent that most of us are apt to forget the past. Men and women do not always remember the supreme fact that once they were children. Such short memory is highly injurious to the teacher. For anger is nearly always the result of incomplete understanding. If one wants to understand a boy, one might do worse than recall one's own boyhood. If the teacher has so completely cut himself off from the days of his boyhood as to be incapable of recollecting at least their more vivid outlines, he should not know a boy when he sees one. He hides his inability to see the living motives in boy-behaviour in an exhibition of anger loftily posed before his pupils. It is part of kind Nature's colour-scheme to provide her creatures with some means or other of disguising their defects and defenceless states and securing, as far and as long as possible, self-protection. And since it is Nature that provides the means, the disguise is not always conscious. The teacher does not usually 'put on the boards' his anger. He simply goes for the class, and he goes for it without much searchings of heart because he does not know the origin of his excitement. He must know it and knowing it, try to keep anger out of the way.

The teacher must have complete hold of himself at all times, firstly, because good teaching demands it, and secondly, because anger would argue a serious imperfection in himself which does not go with real education. Anger is an effervescence that poisons personality, that pollutes that sense of beauty which should be among the highest aims of the teacher to impart to his pupils. It is a wide world we live in and even anger, the accursed, may have a place in it, but in schools where life is sought to be fashioned after the best models, we cannot afford it a place. If not cause, howsoever grave, can put the teacher's 'monkey up', that unrepentant dear thing will lend some of its architectural fancies to the structure that he is trying to build.

Intolerance is a form of anger more dangerous than the plain thing we call temper, because it sometimes wears a seemly look and delivers itself in dignified phrases. Intolerance is a bad word but it always goes about with the scent of some good word or other on it. For example, it now calls itself progress, now conscience, now courage, in fact, anything that has, won a niche in the approbation of men. Religious intolerance is the commonest vice of mankind. It often becomes a habit and sometimes even enters heredity. The teaching profession has a special responsibility resting on it.

Partiality is very often traceable to intolerance. When intolerance becomes bold enough to speak through partiality, the days of its life fortunately are numbered. A powerful teacher may be able to preserve partiality for some time but not for long. When partiality goes down out it usually drags its author along with it. Partiality is very powerful and because it is so it lays hold of some teachers now and then. Intolerance and partiality make themselves attractive by promising a degree of 'influence' to their friends. The intolerant and partial teacher often enjoys the support of some 'class-consciousness' in the school. That is a strange thing to find in any educational institution but it is often found, and is proof of the educational decadence to which we can liable in modern times.

An ounce of partiality is enough to destroy a ton of good teaching. The partial teacher stands condemned in the judgement of the class. He can give no right impulses to his student. He cannot teach who has been 'sacked' by the consciences of his pupils. He may, however, continue to be a teacher to the detriment of the school. When one speaks about partiality, one feels as if one were slinging ink and is eager to stop. What has been said because the existence of partiality in education is not as nearly imaginary as partiality is bad.

Almost all young teachers, new to their work, want to become popular among their pupils. This is not in itself anything bad. The desire for popularity is a good enough thing but genuine popularity which is always seasoned with respect, does not alight on the teacher ready-made from the heavens. It takes him years to get it if he is destined to get it at all. It takes him some work to get it. Popularity untouched with respect is distinctly worse than useless. When a young teacher develops a 'popularity-mania', he employs whatever means is handy to satisfy his craving. He chums up 'with the boys, talks 'shop' with them, tells them tales' out of school'. The 'little beasts' unwilling to cast off their 'little ways' at the bidding of the older teachers adore the new-comer with all their 'little hearts'. It does not take any ability to sell oneself at a cheap price. The ability of the teacher should be proved by his power to elevate his pupils and getting them to like him at the same time. We cannot educate anyone making education all beer and skittles. The 'popularity-mania' induces the teacher to go down to, rather than to raise, his pupils.

It is a well-known fact, in the sense that what is not good easily gets wind, that amity among teachers is more desired and sought than found. As far as teachers are concerned, the thing called resprite de corps or sense of belonging to a community, has often to flourish on occasional dose of lip-service and if it does not factually flourish the cause is known. Teachers have the greatest need to know one another because they work on the same material. If several artists make a piece of sculpture by turns they cannot afford to be ignorant of what their fellows have been doing and how. Intelligent co-operation must be the basis of their work if success is to be attained at all. Yet among teachers, who closely resemble the artists we have been contemplating mutual sympathy and understanding are more often not seen than seen. A sort of secret rivalry would seen to animate the teachers belonging to the same school and often teaching the very same boys. This is very intriguing, to say the least of it.

What might be the reasons? Is it because moving among immature minds they unconsciously imbibe some of the imperections to which these minds are naturally subject? Is it because the spirit of emulation which comes to workers in the same field and perhaps ought to come acted upon by unfavourable circumstances swiftly changes its nature and turns to rivalry? There is no doubt something rotten in the State of Denmark. That something perhaps is the emoluments side of the profession, its commercial competition side, not a good thing to be found in schools at any rate. Of course there are things in the world like currying favour cathing backstair-influence crooking knees and stealing marches. And these are naturally more prominent in stake than in private education a circumstance that makes a strong case against state interference in education wherever the state has not completely dropped its oligarchio character to which all states cling as long and as emotionally as possible. Be it as it may rivalry among teachers is very harmful to education. It intensifies their natural aversion to society which promotes a baneful communalism among them and engenders in them an evil egotism, a spurious individuality, an injurious reluctance to pull well and together which are not quite hospitable to the benefits that education holds out. It must try the teacher to keep fighting always against these many enemies. But to fight against evil is his real job in life and directly he lays down arms he must cease to be teacher.

Regarding discontent it might at once be said that every one is entitled to it provided it is the right sort which is seldom to be had. Discontent is very good if it leads to individual and collective effort to change the state of affairs that gives it rise. The trouble is that discontent seldom does that. The power of discontent lies rather in killing effort and creating gloom. There is gloom enough already in the teaching professional although happily it is yet too early to pronounce effort dead.

No teacher worth his salt can permit charges of discontent and depression go undared. Nothing is easier than to nurse discontent and say that the times are out of joint. The teacher to whom is given the glorious company of young boys and girls just peeping out delightedly into the world can never safely come near the gentle art of making a long face. Nobody has any business to play the skeleton at the feast, and possibly no good can ever come out of the gratuitous part. It is the duty of the teacher to go about his work smiling while sparing no effort to make things better than he finds them. He owes it to himself no less than to the young under his care.

BLESSINGS OF TEACHING

Without straining what is called the sense of proportion it may be said that the noblest of professions and the sorriest of trades is the happiest of vocations. In recent times much has been written about this high and ill-rewarded work—too much, perhaps. Teaching has been drawn in dismal colours and if some of these are found to have been borrowed from truthful sources it has not even then markedly helped in rendering the picture attractive.

Commiseration for the teacher has, therefore, become an easy enough matter and the commiseration is ineffective for the simple reason that it is cheap and nasty as the market jargon goes. It cannot, of course, be denied that there are thorns in teaching as thorns are a supplementary fate of roses, but it cannot also be denied that in teaching there are flower-gardens and fine blossoms too. An almost organic defect of modern thought is that it has a chronic little way of forgetting the other side of the medal.

The condescending pity that seeks to honour the teacher with its attentions is the teacher's worst enemy. It encourages him to commiserate himself, which is about the worst earthly calamity that could befall any individual. It is, therefore, the teacher's prime duty to resist tears where tears are not called. Optimism can often be stupid but a mournful outlook on life exempt from those obligatory impulses and instincts that cunningly persuade us to hitch our little wagons to far off shining things has seldom been discovered a friend of humanity. Even if one were inclined to pessimise one cannot go farther than to say that it is imperative that the teacher must at least try and make the best of a bad bargain.

In former times when education was more or less for the few instruction generally remained in the hands of those who were born with a bent and brought up in the fitness to give it. This is the Indian tradition. These born and self-constituted teachers were honoured and were happy sometimes even more happy than the rest of the community. During the last one hundred years or so education happily has been travelling from the few to the many and today it is asking everyone to come under its umbrella.

The demand for teachers has therefore vastly exceeded the supply of the real article and in satisfying the demand it has not always been found possible to concentrate too much on value. The result is that today in teaching there are workers who have mistaken their vocation as well as those who have found it. Teachers training colleges have stepped forward to make the wrong elements happy and efficient and the right ones happier and more efficient. How far these institutions are justifying expectations still remains a debatable question. However that may be the general consensus of opinion among the majority of teachers if it could be obtained unpolluted by alien considerations will be found to be in favour of voting teaching a nobler profession than a sorry trade. Teaching has certainly its blessings.

In teaching the wrong words subsidizing the wrong ideas have done considerable harm. Teaching has never been and perhaps never can be a profession to say nothing of its being or becoming a trade. Whatever it might be in other professions, the crux of the matter in teaching is the inward call in it the mind ought to be greatly more than money and it is only when the money idea overpowers teaching that it becomes the sorriest of trades at the expense of the noblest of professions. Although money has grown to a size all out of proportion to its intrinsic value in the modern world there remain still certain human efforts which cannot be sustained by the strength of money alone. Mind and spirit where they are honoured still maintain their proud independence of earthly cravings. Gold can lend no glamour to the temple of knowledge nor electricity illuminate its halls. The teacher must really like teaching to be good at it, and he must really be good at it to know its blessings, and to him that is really good at it teaching holds many blessings. And there is comfort for all that are engaged in teaching in the assurance that although the training colleges do not always succeed in making them like the work or in persuading them to reach its highest possibilities they can do these of themselves. It is only those that shut their eyes to the joys of teaching that can neither see them nor have them. There might also be eyes that shut themselves in ignorance. That is the reason why it must be made clear that there are real blessings in teaching to delight such as would have them.

The tragedy of present day school life is that it makes it easy for the teacher to deflect his attention from fundamental things from living needs to a mechanical succession of so-called realities. Yearings and dreams essential elements in life, are forgotten in the uproar of visible things. They are forgotten because it is easier to make a machine than to dream a dream. Subjects have therefore become more important than stimulation and examinations more important than education. In such an atmosphere the teacher must strive for all he is worth even to suspect the joys of teaching. While a just equilibrium between body and soul is the ideal in education what is frequently achieved is the dominance of soul by body. Yes it is easier to feed the body than to nourish the soul. The teacher is thus strongly tempted to remain exiled from the joys of teaching.

There are also other channels to blessing in teaching than the company and contemplation of growing boys and girls. There are varied opportunities for self-improvement in this profession. There is peace and quiet in it, the best of all aids to man to know himself, peace and quiet in which life puts forth its noble blossoms. The imperious haste that marks the march of things in modern times does not happily hamper teaching yet to any great extent. The teacher might still work in an atmosphere of sious in these days enjoy the calm that attaches to teaching. The week's work is crowned by a double holiday inviting the teacher to enrich himself in tranquillity. Long vacations come bearing chance and change. He may renew himself, emerge from active rest another man. Where chances of renewal are not denied there is no monotony. Monotony is the curse of unexercised minds, but every day the call comes to the teacher to catch a new symphony to give the savour of new things to his soul.

It is as difficult as it is easy to be a teacher for long and not to aspire perfection and happiness, for although these lie hidden from the casual eye the awaking ear catches their whispers while the class rooms resound with the time table. The school rules stand at bay against the disobedience of boys and girls and examinations come and go uttering threats and holding out hopes strewing sorrow and joy. Behind the aggressive outward are the true realities. The outward must ask the teacher to go and hang his head in shame. The inward will try and elude him. This is the normal fate of teaching, a sad enough fate which it is absolutely necessary, every teacher must try and escape for the peace of his mind and the glory of his work. If the teacher is the school it is the teacher's inner life that is the only quarry from which to make himself.

There is a spurious mental life, a low intellectual existence which both the teacher and the pupil can live and mistake for the higher thing. It is an insidious lure against which the teacher cannot guard himself or warn his pupils too well. To stir the inner depths of the mind is his great mission and not to sail a fragile craft that cannot live in a single storm on its back waters and call it adventurous cruise. Mind speaks to mind and unless the teacher dives deep and explores his own inner ocean he can not help others do it. It is the teacher that lives the inner life that moves the inner life and knows the joys of teaching. Every blessing is girdled by a belt of barking breakwaters and there is need for some initial venture to brave them.

It is so very important that the teacher must realise the blessings that he might have, for on this realisation not only depends his own happiness but also the ultimate fate of education itself. The personal, the spiritual, element is ninety per cent of instruction. Where education flies its own flag the teacher is all. From him comes inspiration and he gives the word. He must really be the king the ruler whose life is merged in the life of the children he rules. It is not inevitable that the head that wears the educational crown should lie uneasy, but where the true crown is not worn it is almost inevitable that it must often lie very uneasy indeed.

3

PRE-SERVICE TEACHER TRAINING

The modern society needs teachers with different orientation and specialisations to manage educational programmes. The teachers are also needed for physical education, music, art, painting, dance, work education and vocational subjects and for the non-formal stream, distance education, adult education, and open learning system. The scope of teacher education curriculum, therefore, gets enlarged. Therefore, the curriculum for teacher preparation, in future has to emcompass the broader canvas which is consistently emerging before the teachers and shall continue to change at a much faster pace in times ahead.

Teachers shall have to take a global view of the new trends, strategies and practices, and focus on indigenous heritage and thoughts which could fit in the local and national situations. Transplantation of alien educational ideas and practices has not been found rewarding in developing countries. The emerging structures and designs of the curriculum shall lay greater emphasis on the ideas, practices and experiences that have emerged through the contributions of great thinkers.The teacher education programmes shall focus on competencies and commitment in much greater magnitude in future.

OBJECTIVES OF TEACHER EDUCATION

The general objectives of teacher education derived from the contexts, concerns and issues of education, teacher education and the perceived profile of the teacher, could include the following:

— to promote capabilities for inculcating national values and goals as enshrined in the Constitution of India.

— to enable teachers to act as agents of modernisation and social change.

— to sensitise teachers towards the promotion of social cohesion, international understanding and protection of human rights and rights of the child.

— to transform student-teachers into competent and committed professionals willing to perform the identified tasks.

— to develop competencies and skills needed for becoming an effective teacher.

— to sensitise teachers and teacher educators about emerging issues, such as environment, ecology, population, gender equality, legal literacy, etc..

— to empower teachers to cultivate rational thinking and scientific temper among students.

— to develop critical awareness about the social realities.

— to develop managerial and organisational skills.

PROFILE OF A TEACHER

The profile of a teacher which emanates from the contexts and concerns necessarily implies additional roles besides the conventional ones. The following capabilities and competencies need to be highlighted:

— inculcating the intrinsic and extrinsic values of professional competency, professional commitment and professional ethics,

— creating and reconstructing knowledge,

— selecting, organising and using learning resources,

— effectively transacting curriculum, selecting and organising educational activities and programmes for learners with special needs,

— using media and appropriate instructional technologies,

— communicating effectively and responding to the challenges of continuity and change,

— counselling students for personality development, adjustment and learning attainment,

— conducting research, especially action research and initiating innovative practices,

— organising student-activities,

— inculcating a sense of value judgement, value commitment and value transmission,

— understanding the importance of inter-relationship between culture and education and 'culture and personality,

— fostering interest in life-long learning,

— understanding the aspirations and expectations of the community and establishing mutually supportive linkages between school and community,

— acting as a change agent for modernisation and development.

The educational programmes for prospective teachers, therefore, need to be so designed as to develop in them the requisite potential and capabilities.

CURRICULUM FRAMEWORK

The perceived characteristics of the envisaged curriculum framework would include the following:

- — reflects the Indian heritage, acts as an instrument in the realisation of national goals and fulfills aspirations of people.
- — responds to the latest developments in the field of education.
- — establishes integration of theory and practice of education.
- — provides multiple educational experiences to teachers.
- — enables teachers to experiment with new ideas.
- — ensures inseparability of pre-service and in-service education of teachers.
- — sets achievable goals for various stages of teacher education.
- — provides for use of communication technology.

PREPEARING TEACHERS FOR EARLY CHILDHOOD

In order to provide healthy and enriched childhood to young learners, a new type of teacher specifically sensitised about the perspectives of child development will be required. In order that early childhood education becomes a reality, in terms of its organisation and accessibility, one of the significant inputs in making a success story of it is that of a professionally trained and committed teacher. The professional preparation of teachers for this stage, hitherto unplanned and uncared for, calls for thoughtful planning of training sequences relevant to the developmental needs of early childhood interwoven with commonalities and specificities.

The programmes for early childhood education have been launched under Integrated Child Development Scheme through Anganwadis, Day Care Centres, Balwadies, Pre-primary Schools run by the State Governments, Municipal Corporations, Voluntary Agencies and Private Agencies. All such efforts, though not adequately provided for, are continuing with diverse approaches without making a synergic impact. Concerted efforts are needed for organising early childhood education in a planned manner. It presupposes pooling of resources by the community as well as the concerned agencies.

The objectives of teacher education specific to early childhood include the following:

- to prepare teachers for facilitating physical, mental, moral, social, aesthetic and linguistic development of children,
- to acquaint them with the knowledge of child psychology,
- to cultivate social sensitivity, affection for children and respect for their uniqueness,
- to acquaint them with techniques of caring for children and enable them to identify their needs,
- to provide experiences and organise activities that promote children's self-concept, creativity and inventiveness,
- to enable them to select, prepare and use different kinds of resource materials,
- to develop a sense of involvement with and appreciation of local resources and their utilisation,
- to develop an acquaintance with basics of Scientific and Technological Literacy,
- to develop a repertoire of children's games, songs and literature,

— to empower student-teachers towards creating learning readiness among young learners.

No formal teaching is visualised at early childhood stage. It is not a stage for introducing three R's. In the preparation of teachers for this stage, therefore, the main thrust will be on sensitising prospective teachers about change and its implications—cultural, social, economic, etc. as also with the change in the learner through motivation and learning.

Future need will be to empower the teacher to observe change, interpret it and adopt, adapt, modify, consolidate, accelarate or reject the same. It is not intended here to suggest details of progrmmes and theoretical content. It is, however, expected that the course on Emerging Indian Society will enable the intending teachers to know about the rights of child, human rights, legal literacy, community dynamics, knowledge of national and local festivals, emerging trends in community life and social living, prominent personalities in various walks of life, familiarity with factors and forces affecting environmental and population equilibirium, knowledge and appreciation of places of historical and cultural significance and landmarks and trends of development.

Another theoretical input which is intended to be given to the prospective teachers is regarding knowledge of nature and scope, status, problems and issues concerning early childhood education in India. These need to be understood in terms of Indian reality and perspective, foundations of child behaviour etc. In addition, it may include, among others, progress of early childhood education, its historical development, problems, need for looking at it from the point of view of diversity, flexibility, local relevance and specificities, and the agencies involved in the process of promoting early childhood education.

Basic to designing programmes and activities for children at this stage is a thorough understanding of various aspects of growth and development of the child which the prospective teachers will be required to internalise. Since, it is being recommended for intending teachers of pre-schoolers, it will be necessary to know about the fundamentals of early childhood care and education.

Most of the training programmes of teachers for this stage will have major concentration on organisation and activities. In addition, the teachers will be required to have a practical training at early childhood education centres and the like. At this stage, greater emphasis will be given on propagation of early childhood care.

Transacting Developmentally Appropriate Curriculum

India is a conglomeration of diversities with a variety of manifestations and yet bound by a thread of commonality. Teacher is expected to recognise commonalities and specificities in order to shape the personality of children for living together in a perpetually changing complex society.

The suggested theoretical components included in the framework are essentially, meant for broadening the intellectual horizons of intending teachers who will become conversant with the culture and traditions of the country with due appreciation of the diversities. The seeds of democratic living are sown from the beginning of childhood and education needs to be regarded as a vehicle for maintaining equilibirium in the growth of individuals from childhood to adulthood.

It would be worth experimenting with modular approach of teaching combined with interventions of realistic nature by way of field trips, visit to museums, zoo, educational excursions, visit to mountains, forests, intermediary interventions with real life situations and through audio-video devices, wherever possible. Teaching in teacher training institutions be directed towards empowering prospective teachers to enable to use their experiences in actual work places for enhancing growth and development of young children.

There is to be a planned amalgam of theory and practice in a way that these two constitute a continuum of experiences. The teaching of theoretical components will combine various methods and approaches like lecturing, tutorials, seminars, term-papers, discussion groups, gaming, role planning, etc.

The teachers at this stage are being initiated into and introduced to the art of teaching. Teaching to them is romance with innovativeness and inventiveness. It is love for children. It is caring for children. It is seeking for optimum enrichment of experiences of children. It is providing happiness to children. It is making their stay joyful in schools.

The early childhood education includes transacting developmentally appropriate curriculum which includes within its fold concept development, convergent and divergent thinking, creative activities, language acquisition, etc. It is an arduous task of equipping prospective teachers with competencies and skills needed for making the learning experiences of a child joyful and memorable. It must be admitted that the training of pre-school teachers is complex and full of challenges.

The pedagogical aspects of training will be planned around activities and programmes for children, attending to their needs, identifying interests of learners by gender and their background, identifying children with special needs and devising strategies for their optimum growth and development, organising games, recreational activities, plays, etc.

Theory and practicals have to be linked and integrated in the training process. Much of what goes by way of practicals is intrinsically related with pedagogy and much of the essence of pedagogy lies in the practical work. The practical work may include comprehensive case studies of children including children with special needs, gifted children, children coming from different socio-economic and cultural backgrounds, etc.

Development and use of schedules, assessment checklists and other evaluation tools and techniques will form an important aspect of practicum. The maximum utilisation of environmental and community resources can be done only when the teacher is thoroughly conversant with environmental resources. Community survey, therefore, is one of the several activities of practical work which requires systematic exploration.

The practical work of the prospective teachers will centre around evolving and devising programmes and activities for physical, psychomotor, cognitive, emotional and other aspects of development. Health and hygiene, habit formation, are certain other areas which require practical work. In addition, art, drawing and painting, using clay/plasticin, music, dance, recreation, story telling, games, and physical activity are a variety of examples of other practical experiences which a student teacher will be required to undertake for creative expression of children.

Evaluation for the theoretical component may include assessment of sessional work, term-papers, participation in seminars, discussion groups, etc. besides semester examinations which can be oral, written, practical and objective type. The written tests have to be reliable, valid and representative of the totality of experiences. Different tools and techniques of evaluation can be used for assessing the pupils' growth. Visits to and partcipation in activities of Anganwadis, Balwadis, Day Care Centres will make a part of training towards understanding the dynamics of working with children and educating them.

The evaluation of this component will be in the form of a cumulative record of the performance of the intending teachers. External evaluation of practical activities will defeat the purpose as the practical work is, by and large, activity-based. It is essentially sessional work, day-to-day internal assessment, feed back and monitoring. A record of some of the activities is all that may be suggested for purposes of evaluation in this regard.

TEACHER PREPERATION FOR PRIMARY EDUCATION

The formulation of curriculum framework for primary stage (classes I to V) has been guided by general and specific objectives of teacher education and perceived characteristics of curriculum development. The specific objectives of primary teacher education may include the following:

— to develop understanding of the psychological and sociological foundations relevant to the primary stage.

— to enable teachers to manage appropriate resources for organising learning experiences of children.

— to acquaint them with methods and techniques of caring for children with special needs.

— to enable them to acquire necessary skills so as to develop curiosity, imagination and creativity.

— to develop in them the capacity to understand and analyse the social and emotional problems.

— to develop communication skills

— to enable them to establish mutually supportive linkages with the community focussing on the objective of UPE/UEE.

— to enable them to understand implications of research for teaching-learning and undertake action research and use innovative practices.

— to enable them to organise games, sports, physical activities and other co-curriculur activities.

The teacher needs to be empowered through training inputs to gain greater insights into the complexities of the society and the historical perspective of the developmental process. Themes on Emerging Indian Society should be introduced at this stage with a purpose of making the teacher aware of the contextual realities in which he or she has to work. It takes into account rights of children, human rights education, values and their broad features, perspectives of educational, social, economic and political development in the country, significant landmarks in the process of development in various fields including science and technology, etc.

Theoretical component is essential for understanding the learner, community and the society, the internal and external forces impinging upon the school and the internal and external variables operating upon the learner. The inclusion of Courses on Psychology of Teaching and Learning, Health and Physical Education, Education of Children with Special Needs has been made for accommodating this point of view in the Framework.

In the proposed training programmes, the prospective teachers would be imparted training in a manner that theory and practice are organically integrated. Correlation within the curricular areas of learning and external environment is established. Psychology of Teaching and Learning, School Organisation and Pedagogical Analysis of primary school subjects will provide a sound base for the adoption of integrated approach to teaching and learning and for establishing meaningful and interactive bonds between theory and practice. The intent of including Action Research and Education of Children with Special Needs is guided by the fact that every student-teacher is expected to know the elements of action research, surveys, community services etc and is capable of educating children with special needs. Additional areas may be included for making the course content relevant and region specific.

Transactional Strategies

Transactional strategies invariably need to emphasise interactive, partcipative and activity-oriented approach. The transaction of curriculum will have place to place and intra-and inter-content variations. The theoretical component of the curriculum can be transacted by lecture-discussion, self-study approach, seminars, media supported teaching wherever possible, tutorials and through practical activities. It is expected that the intending teachers during the course of training acquire mastery of competencies and skills that are basic to making an effective, reflective and committed teacher.

Practice teaching remains to be a weak link of curriculum transaction. This point of view has been substantiated and re-inforced by field surveys conducted by NCTE at different places throughout the country. In this framework, pedagogical analysis of school teaching subjects has been thought of as an essential component of practice teaching. By way of pedagogical analysis a student teacher becomes conversant with the objectives of teaching a unit, the entry behaviour of pupils, classroom management and evaluation strategies. With this background of having looked into the pedagogical aspects of school teaching subjects, the student teacher is likely to become more effective and confident in his/her interventions in the classroom.

As a necessary part of the training of primary school teachers, knowledge of content is given due importance during the course of training. Mastery of subject matter, the insight gained through pedagogical analysis and the foundation courses when thoughtfully integrated and used for classroom instruction will lead to improving the quality of education.

Practical work is an essential component for internalising the theoretical concepts. Thus it will have to be planned on each aspect of theoretical inputs. In addition, practical activities centring around different school experiences, work education, school community interaction, action research projects and other educational activities directed towards development of personality of students will also be undertaken by intending teachers. It needs continuous planning, analysing, monitoring and evaluation throughout the duration of the course which will necessitate the involvement of teacher educators more vigorously than what it is presently.

It is expedient to employ the formative evaluation for obtaining continuous feedback, motivating students and guiding their efforts. There is an increasing felt need to replace external examinations by internal continuous and comprehensive examination system. External system of evaluation, until such times it is replaced, may be perceived as a corrective, moderating and balancing factor. It, therefore, needs to be carefully planned and testing tools made valid and reliable. In different situations evaluation of theoretical component may be based on essay questions, short answer type questions, objective type questions, objective-based questions, oral examinations, participation in discussion groups etc.

Evaluation of practice teaching can be done internally, externally or through judicious combination of both. Gradual transition to continuous and comprehensive internal evaluation of practice teaching and assigning grades instead of marks would be a professionally sound step. Evaluation of practical work would also be done internally.

PREPEARING TEACHERS FOR ELEMENTARY EDUCATION

The formulation of the curriculum framework for the elementary stage will also be guided by general and specific objectives of teacher education and characteristics of curriculum development. The specific objectives relevant to the stage may include the following:

— to develop understanding of the psychological and sociological principles relevant to elementary stage of education.

— to enable teachers to select, prepare and use appropriate resources for organising learning experiences.

— to acquaint them with methods and materials of teaching children with special needs

— to develop among them the capacity to solve the social and emotional problems of children.

— to enable them acquire necessary skills so as to develop curiosity, imagination and self-confidence among children.

— to develop communication skills

— to enable them to mobilise and utilise community resources as educational inputs.

— to enable them to organise supplementry educational activities

— to undertake action research projects

— to enable them to establish mutually supportive linkages with the community

— to enable them to organise games, sports, physical activities and other co-curricular activities.

The course on Emerging Indian Society will enable the prospective teachers to understand the demands that society expects education to fulfil. Similarly, proposed course on 'Elementary Education in India—Status, Problems and Issues' will promote the capacity to examine if these expectations can really be met. The course on Psychology of Teaching and Learning will teach them how to formulate their teaching strategies to promote learning among children. Health and Physical Education will enable them to plan exercises for development of sound physiques of formative evaluation. They will be able to deal with children with special needs and adopting problem solving approach, a capacity built by Action Research. The course on counselling and guidance will enable them to help children when they are confronted with problem of any kind.

The pedagogical analysis will provide the prospective teachers an understanding of the complexity involved in the teaching of the subjects at the elementary level. This will enable them to plan their educational strategies. A critical observation of model lessons and practice teaching in the actual class room situation will make them effective and competent teachers. Internship in a school will offer the prospective teachers the varied experiences needed for working in a school. They will internalise educational value of the work and experience the dignity of manual work. The school community interaction would not only promote the interactive support between both but also enable them to evolve suitable pedagogy for children. The organisation of education activities will develop the capacity for planning and undertaking such activities as are essential for the development of personalty of the student. The theoretical and practical courses suggested in this frame are capable of preparing a competent elementary school teacher.

Transactional Strategies

The prospective teachers are to be prepared as to enable them to perform successfully in the pre-instructional, instructional and post-instructional phases of teaching. For this, several well-designed approaches like lecture discussion cooperative study, self-study and project methods etc. may be adopted. Depending on the nature of the subject, the teachers may combine different strategies and instructional aids, utilise media supported teaching, organise field trips and practicals and demonstration techniques. In this process due attention be given to children with special needs. The curriculum transaction will have to be adjusted with the needs of students and locally available resources.

During the process of teaching and learning, the existing transactional strategies marginally promote the capacity for independent study, self-discovery and self-study and rarely seek prospective teachers' participation and remain one way traffic with the result that the subject matter communicated is partially assimilated and not fully utilised. Teacher education has to inculcate professional commitment, develop competencies and make teacher reflective to deal with specific situations.

Practice teaching, the weakest link of teacher education, possesses the potentiality of converting itself into a strong component if properly organised. The process of curriculum transaction needs improvement and enrichment. Pedagogical analysis of teaching subjects is sure to refine teaching and learning as it will transform the teachers' performance and develop competencies not covered by the method-cum-content approach. With the background of pedagogical analysis and model and demonstration lessons given by the teacher educator, the class room performance is sure to improve if it is supervised in detail by the subject specialist.

Work education is an important component of practical work and its potentiality has to be utilised by teacher education for developing certain qualities of character. Community surveys helps to formulate a proper social perspective. The mutually supported school and community interaction helps the teachers to evolve suitable teaching strategies. The teachers will be required to organise educational activities in school. They have to learn to plan and organise such activities as are essential to provide opportunities for self-expression and lead to development of personality of students. They have to be trained for utilising supplementary materials essential for accelerating and promoting learning among students.

The teachers will be required to facilitate physical, social, emotional and aesthetic development of students. Their creative and constructive potentialities have to be fostered. Practical activities suggested in the document will help to achieve these ends. It is, therefore, necessary to organise these activities on continuing basis. The influence of teachers' personality and behaviour has lasting impact on students. In the selection and adoption of transactional strategies the teacher has to ensure that teaching becomes participatory, cooperative, activity-centred and joyful.

The success or failure of the curriculum transaction is ascertained by evaluation done by means of valid and reliable tools. At this stage, evaluation has to be continuous, formative and comprehensive to bring improvement in teaching learning process. Systematic evaluation will enable a teacher to select proper teaching strategies and effect suitable changes in the curriculum process. The evaluation of the pupil teachers at the elementary stage will not differ much from the primary stage and the same principles and similar practices which have been adopted at the primary level may be utilised at this stage.

PREPEARING TEACHERS FOR SECONDARY CLASSROOMS

For teaching at secondary stage, the qualification most sought after is one year B.Ed. which is in fact B.Ed. for secondary stage. However, at present, there are several variations for first degree level qualification which are also available. These include B.Ed. (Elementary); B.Ed. (Special Education); which too are programmes of one year duration; B.Ed. through correspondence or distance education mode which is now of two years duration. There are certain other variations in the form of vacation courses or part-time courses which were available before NCTE norms came into force. In addition, there are four-year integrated courses for elementary stage and also for secondary stage. Teacher education programme at this stage, like at all other stages, will include the theory, practice teaching in schools, and practical work in the light of contexts, concerns, profile of teachers and general and specific objectives.

The specific objectives at this stage may include the following:

— to enable the prospective teachers to understand the nature, purpose and philosophy of secondary education.

— to develop among teachers an understanding of the psychology of their pupils.

— to enable them to understand the process of socialisation.

— to equip them acquire competencies relevent to stage specific pedagogy, curriculum development, its transaction and evaluation.

— to enable them to make pedagogical analysis of the subjects they are to teach at the secondary stage.

— to develop skills for guidance and counselling.

— to enable them to foster creative thinking among pupils for reconstruction of knowledge.

— to acquaint them with factors and forces affecting educational system and class room situation.

— to acquaint them with educational needs of special groups of pupils.

— to enable them to utilise community resources as educational inputs.

— to develop communication skills and use the modern information technology.

— to develop aesthetic sensibilities.

— to acquaint them with research in education including action research

A teacher helps in improving the quality of human life in the context of multiple internal and external forces impinging on man and the society. The course on Emerging Indian Society, would develop an insight into the nature of Indian society, its variety and complexities and making teacher education programme relevant to the community. Ingenuity of teachers lies in first understanding national ethos and then planning for teaching within this framework as a professional. A professionally trained teacher is expected to identify the strengths and weaknesses of secondary education in India and after having gained insights into the status, problems and issues concerning education at this stage, develop a mental make-up of evaluating the system and utilising the same for promoting excellence in education.

A teacher in the classroom has to make adjustments in teaching strategy according to the nature and scope of the curriculum and evaluate the success of teaching in terms of students' growth. The foundations of curriculum, pedagogy, evaluation and remediation need to be laid down firmly during the course of professional preparation of teachers. What kind of pedagogical strategy will give optimum results in specific units of curriculum and in what ways the outcomes need to be evaluated will be the main thrust.

Distinct departure from the existing programme is noticeable in including a course on psychology of teaching and learning. The teaching of educational psychology to the B.Ed. trainees was done extensively even earlier but without establishing linkages with actual teaching and learning. The attempt to put teaching and learning together does not in any way undermine the importance of educational psychology. Now the basic thrust will be on teaching—learning processes, group dynamics, learners' background, the internal and external forces of the institution and the community. Psychology of teaching and learning would require adjustments at different levels of schooling and for different grade levels. Foundation courses lend support to refining the education processes implicit in teaching and learning. Comparative perspective of educational systems in developing and developed countries would enable teachers to acquire a global vision of contemporary context and gain greater insight into ways of improving the quality of education.

The understanding of some specific areas of education in detail and in depth is needed for becoming an effective teacher. Guided by this consideration and having been supported through field interactions with different target groups, courses on pre-school education and elementary school education have been included as optionals. Teachers will also be required to get indepth understanding of areas like non-formal alternatives to school education. Similarly avenues for indepth studies in emerging areas of concern like vocational education, environmental education, population education etc. have also been suggested.

The message of educational technology has to reach the classrooms in the form of its application. Prospective teacher has to be so equipped in the course of training as to enable him to think of using appropriate educational technology for improving the quality of instruction and for obtaining optimum results in terms of the students' growth.

Physical education has been considered as an integral part of education. In each system of schooling tremendous amount of emphasis is laid upon building up the cognitive base of students and the affective and psychomotor dimensions of human personality, do not receive adequate attention. A teacher fashioned in the culture of physical education would be conscious of catering to the physical dimension of human personality with concern. The inclusion of this course, however, may not be taken as an alternative to preparing teachers for teaching Physical Education.

Transactional Strategies

The impact of teacher training programmes has not been perceptible over the years in terms of transacting curriculum in schools. Lecture method, mostly taken recourse to by teacher educators, is generally not supplemented by using instructional materials. Interactive teaching, co-operative teaching-learning, self-discovery approaches seldom find place in the day-to-day teaching practices. What is of importance and calls for top priority in the training programme, is to lay appropriately proportioned emphasis on 'why to teach', 'how to teach' and 'what to teach' aspects of teaching. It has to be reflected in the teaching-learning situations planned by teacher educators.

Education as a field of specialised studies is inter-disciplinary in its nature. Since different branches of learning are involved in understanding process and product variables of education, it is essential that formulation of teacher education programmes adopts a holistic approach in order to promote proper understanding, insight and thinking on matters pertaining to this field. The complimentary character of theory and practice needs to be emphasised at every step. The prospective teachers are encouraged to organise, express and communicate their ideas clearly in the class. It has to be accepted as a communicative process of an intensive teacher-learner dialogue and renewal of a two-way process as opposed to 'the banking concept' of teaching. The emphasis must be laid on cultivation, formation and development of power of mind in contrast to the prevalent tendency of aiming at the success in examination alone. Student-teachers, it is hoped, in classroom transactions, will employ the use of divergent thinking and problem solving strategy.

The teacher educators will be required to have clarity of thought in respect of components of a course, objectives of teaching, and their relevance to educational and social goals. One of the approaches may be the modular approach. Each module, though a complete teaching unit, remains a part of the total syllabus with built-in linkages and feedback mechanisms. Learning through this approach can be reinforced by library work, seminar readings, tutorials and small group discussions. Self-study and self-motivated learning become an integral part of the curriculum transaction. The outcomes would result in better understanding of concepts better leading to mastery learning.

The interdisciplinary approach in teaching has to be accepted and implemented for developing comprehensive understanding and vision of educational studies. Learning outcomes have to be assessed continuously, which is the basic tenet of the modular approach. This would help in modifying, adjusting and improving transaction strategies for better acquisition of knowledge. Universities have options to evolve their own examination system. Too much reliance on external examinations, however, would inhibit the progress of moving in the direction of quality education.

Student Teaching and Practical Activities

There is no denying the fact that practice of education is as important as its theory. Each good theory leads to a good practice and vice-versa. To strike a balance between theory and the practice of education, therefore, is a matter of judicious planning and scheduling in order to give proper direction to teacher education. Changes in the pattern and practices of student teaching have been only peripheral. The content-cum-method approach, wherever attempted, remained limited to the introduction of an additional component of content without fully achieving the objective of integration. The problem-solving approach, discovery method, competency based teaching learning and the indigenous contributions, like those of Gandhi, Tagore, Aurobindo, Zakir Hussain and several others have the potential for bringing in innovative ideas in teacher education. The application of educational technology, informatics, telematics, cybernetics etc. have yet to make a discernible headway. The learning resources wherever available in the training institutions and the community as also in the schools have not been optimally utilised.

Prerequisite to preparing a prospective teacher can be thought of in terms of providing certain inputs such as, induction programme, an exposure of school experiences with special focus on the educational environment of the school, socio-economic and cultural background of the community constituting the catchment area, observation of classroom teaching and other related activities etc. Induction programme might include acquainting the intending teachers with the school settings, the school programmes—curricular and co-curricular. In addition, they will be prepared for actual classroom teaching and the roles they are expected to assume during the course of practice teaching/internship by way of focussed discussions, demonstration lessons, preparation of lesson plans in a way as to encompass teaching for cognitive, affective and psychomotor development.

Practice teaching is essentially a joint responsibility of teacher training institution and the school involving teacher educators, prospective teachers and school teachers. Teacher educators will help in facilitating and guiding the activities as implied by the pre-instructional, instructional and post-instructional phases through which a student teacher has to progress. The role of a school teacher in this joint effort lies in extending cooperation to the teacher educator and the intending teacher. Various aspects will have to be suitably adapted to varying structures and designs at different stages of teacher education.

Practical work other than classroom instruction can be viewed in terms of school and community experiences and activities related to personality and leadership development. Efforts need to be directed towards developing in a teacher trainee certain competencies and skills which would be helpful in the shaping of a teacher for effective role play. It is essentially directed towards capacity building which may embrace, among other competencies, managerial skills , organisational efficiency, leadership skills, democratic attitudes, innovative and creative abilities etc.

The teachers' role, which they will be required to play in the school situation other than classroom teaching, may extend to a variety of activities, such as, maintenance of school records and registers, management of laboratories and library, preparation, repair and selection of instructional aids and equipments, selection and preparation of textual materials, preparation of tests and assignments, admission and selection of students, maintenance of progress reports of students, preparation of school budget and development plans, beautification of school and classroom management etc. The institutional activities within the school environs may include dramatic clubs, stage activities, literary activities, inter-house activities and sports and games, organisation of educational tours, etc.

Community Experiences

Interaction between the institution and community is gaining importance in the modern context. One can think of several activities promoting school-community relationship, such as, celebration of birthdays of children, celebration of parents' day, activating parent-teacher association for the welfare of the schools, organisation of school and community games, sports and other functions, utilisation of community resources for education, understanding the background of children, celebration of national days in collaboration with the community, environmental education , adult literacy, plantation and social forestry.

Likewise, community involvement and school development activities may lead to community awareness generating competency through community-institution interaction activities; mobilising community resources for organising literacy programmes, environmental education, work education programme, health awareness programmes, etc. It is expected that organisation of such activities would lead to developing self confidence and initiative among student teachers and also develop among them positive attitude towards plurality of cultures.

The modalities to be employed for organising activities other than teaching for all round capacity building and empowerment of a teacher-trainee will involve joint supervision by the teacher educator and a school teacher. The transaction modes, for example, for motivating adults for making them literate can be through mass participation, folk songs, street plays etc. The identification of various sports and a variety of activities for cleanliness in the community, collecting success stories and disseminating them in the community, preparing simple write-ups of all the activities undertaken; utilising community resources for the developmental needs of library building, students scholarships, awards, student aid funds, celebration of festivals etc; student-parent-community contact programmes and organisation of welfare shows for better institution-community participation are certain other strategies of transaction of practical work.

It is expected that a student-teacher undertakes several practical activities which facilitate instruction as also those that relate to management. Relevant to teaching and learning, the intending teacher develops competencies, like identification of support material, skills in preparation of indigenous and low-cost materials, judicious choice and utilisation of material for enhancing the learning and use of community resources for education. The likely activities may include preparation of an inventory of community resources, instructional material, development of software and use of hardware. The teacher-trainee also gets acquainted with the techniques of diagnosis, remediation, guidance and counselling, classroom interaction inclusive of understanding of context variables implicit in the process of teaching and learning, knowledge of educational rules and regulations/laws, in addition to maintenance of cumulative and comprehensive evaluation records, maintenance of school records and is conscious of professional accountability and ethics. It is hoped that most of the activities will be undertaken by the teacher trainee during the internship period of a reasonable duration. Some of these activities will have to be integrated with practice teaching. For meaningful organisation of practical work pre-internship stage may be utilised for demonstration lessons, lectures, simulation, role- playing, micro-teaching etc.

The transactional mode of community related practical work may include interaction between school teacher and intending teacher and members of the community representing parents, panchayats, senior citizens, voluntary organisations, etc. Student-teachers may undertake a case study of a school (generally a practising school) for identifying its strengths and weaknesses, needs and problems, specific learning problems, such as, drop-outs, drug abuse, behavioural problems, learning difficulties etc. Street plays can be organised by the student teachers to sensitise the community in the ways in which community resources could be utilised and also motivate the community members for greater participation in the school welfare activities.

Work Education

Work education is a powerful medium for personality development. There can be a variety of activities which are necessarily school based and which may be included under work education like maintenance of the school plant including its playgrounds, cleanliness, repair of furniture and production of material to be used as instructional aids. It will be a great educational experience if community visit, field work, nature study, school co-operatives saving bank, games and sports and other co-curricular activities are carefully organised as part of the programmes leading to development of qualities needed for the success of work education.

MORAL EDUCATION

The rapid erosion of values in the society is causing concern, necessitating imparting of moral education. It is generally agreed that cognition is basic to volition which by implication would mean that prospective teachers are expected to understand critical issues regarding values—concept, types, and problems involved in imbibing the values. It is also expected of them to be well-versed with the values enshrined in our Constitution and the values that have the cultural contexts and can be derived from our heritage. In the process of capacity building of intending teachers, what is of importance is to ensure that they become capable of understanding the import of value education, interpreting values in the contemporary contexts and evolving strategies of imbibing these by their students.

Duration to Transact the Curriculum

Through the national consultations initiated by the NCTE, a strong consensus emerged in favour of enhancing the duration of B.Ed. programme from one year to two years. The new curriculum frame not only transforms the nature and content of the traditional foundation courses but also includes several additional components. Emerging Indian Society will deal with factors and forces operating in the Indian society leading to the emergence of a new social order. The psychology of teaching and learning has been given a new thrust. It will also include findings of researches in life sciences, medicine, neurology, genetics and communication technology having their relevance for teaching and learning. A new course on Secondary Education has been included to provide deeper understanding of issues related to secondary education. Likewise, Guidance and Counselling has been incorporated to make teachers more functional in their jobs.

The course on Curriculum Design and Development will promote the capacity of curriculum development evaluation and transaction. A component of Assessment, Evaluation and Remediation has been added. The school management has been incorporated as a compulsory course because all the teachers must possess its knowledge and acquire its techniques. A new component of action research has been included to develop the problem solving approach. Comparative education has been added to broaden outlook of student teachers and to develop their insight into educational problems and issues.

A number of optional subjects out of which the students will select only two has been suggested in the frame. These optionals are intended to develop certain additional competencies among the prospective teachers. The whole spectrum of theoretical courses has therefore not only been enriched but also given a professional shape and outlook which cannot be achieved within the short period of one year.

The practice teaching is now not merely confined to the teaching of certain subjects. Pedagogical analysis of the subjects offered for practice teaching has been made compulsory. The prospective teacher will analyse the subject before going to class and evolve a need-based pedagogy and transactional strategy. The teacher educators will now deliver model lessons of different types in actual classroom situation and the prospective teachers will not only learn the techniques but make its critical appraisal and evaluation to be subsequently discussed with the teachers. Teacher educators supervising the classroom performance, pupil teachers will discuss their observations with them for providing proper feedback to improve their performance. The practice teaching will, thus, require thorough preparation, detailed supervision and adequate time. Its gain would be acquisition of higher level of teaching competencies.

The practical work has been made comprehensive and meaningful. Internship programme shall be enriched to provide all the experience that a teacher needs. After completion of the period of internship the prospective teacher will acquire necessary experiences for working in school and the training received would be complete as against the partial one at present. The implementation of internship in this format will also need increased duration.

The field work, community interaction, school community relationship and similar programme will enable the pupil teacher to develop a need based pedagogy. The organisation of physical education and the educational activities, work education, sessional and practical work related to practice teaching and optional, the formulation of programmes for the development of personality, creativity and aesthetic sensibility and action research will lead to the promotion of skills and competencies needed for a teacher. The practical activities will enhance the competence of the teachers. The duration of the B.Ed. pogramme will therefore have to be increased.

Besides these, a perceptible change in the pedagogy of teacher education itself has been suggested. Its centrality has shifted from the training colleges to schools and its transactional strategies have been transformed. The teacher educators have to make pedagogical analysis of the subjects to be taught and achieve integration between the theory and practice and also the methodology of teaching. They are expected to evolve a culture-specific and need-based pedagogy and develop the potentiality needed for independent learning and self study for which a number of suggestions have been made. The lessons will have to be supervised intensively and formative approach has to be adopted. The teacher educator has now to devote more time in the preparation and planning of his own activities for the professional uplift of the prospective teachers by developing certain additional competencies. All these demand more rigour and need more time.

Professionalism involves its own compulsion and pressure. It needs a change in attitudes and value systems of the teachers. They have to earn social sanction from the community by improving the quality of their work. The scope of teacher education has been enlarged. Teachers have to perform many additional roles in society. Apart from teaching, they have to act as the agent of change and modernisation, cultural reconstruction and social development to earn recognition as a professional from the society by acquiring new competencies and commitment. They have to become effective and result oriented to enhance their knowledge and develop skills for its communication. These are not possible to be achieved within the short span of one year. Hence the need to increase the duration of the present B.Ed. programme from one year to two years. Existing programmes of two years duration leading to Bachelor's degree in education like B.P.Ed. may continue to be of the same duration.

PREPARING TEACHERS FOR SENIOR SECONDARY STAGE

Teacher education programmes have to respond to three major determinants: the stage-specific developmental characteristics of the students, the courses of study they pursue and the academic qualifications the prospective teachers possess. At the Senior Secondary stage all the three become distinctly different from that of the secondary schools which offer a common curriculum upto class ten. The main features of the three determinants are given below:

The development of students at this stage, the later part of adolescence, is characterised by:

— maturity of body and brain

— development of abstract thinking and logic; goal fixation and symbolisation

— self-consciousness, self-identity and self-assertion

— sex-consciousness and sex interest

— personal preferences and choices and ideal formation and differentiation

— peer group influences, strong likes and dislikes, reactions and adventurism

— changes in reference group, imitation of adult behaviour and roles and a tendency of defiance

— moral reasoning and challenging attitude towards the established ideas, practices and authority

— self-esteem and ego-involvement

— attachment to friends

— self-defence and self-exhibition

— argumentation and rebelliousness

— fixation of ideas, development of aptitudes and demarcation of academic or vocational preferences.

Course of Study

For the students of +2 stage, two types of courses—

academic and vocational—have been designed. The characteristics of courses responding to the above are mentioned below:

— *Academic Stream*

  — differentiated, demarcated and specific contents
  — subject and discipline orientation preparatory to specialisation
  — enriched and comprehensive curriculum with goal specificity
  — regrouping of subjects into compulsory and optionals
  — emphasis on abstract and creative thinking and higher mental faculties to deal with complex ideas and complicated concepts.
  — directed and focussed towards higher studies

— *Vocational Stream:* The main characteristics of vocational courses are in their being:

  — job oriented,
  — skill based,
  — useful,
  — practical,
  — manipulative,
  — rich in economic values,
  — employment or self-employment oriented,
  — terminal in nature, and
  — suitable for middle level workers in economy.

The teachers of academic stream require the following :

— enriched and higher academic qualifications and standards
— additional teaching competencies

— different curriculum transactional strategies and modalities

— competency to promote desire for pursuing higher studies and develop academic interests and pursuit of independent study.

To deal with vocational subjects different kinds of teachers are required. They must possess:

— expertise in a vocational subject;

— capacity to inculcate workmanship and dignity of labour;

— ability to transfer skills from one trade/vocation to another;

— competencies to explain scientific principles involved in a trade or vocation;

— capability to impart knowledge and skills for achieving success in a trade or vocation;

— desire to produce an educated citizen, not only a narrow specialist or trade's man;

— ability to inspire students for the constant upgrading of their skills; and

— an understanding of the interrelationship between culture and a vocation.

At present there exists a common programme for the education of teachers for the secondary and senior secondary schools. It is undifferentiated and generalised. But the courses at the senior secondary stage have been enriched. Their nature and goals are dufferent. They have been divided into two broad streams. The characteristics of students have also changed. Under these circumstances certain additional competencies are needed for teachers teaching at this stage. Hence the separate programmes for the academic and vocational streams of teachers.

Academic Stream

An understanding of emerging Indian society and factors and forces operating behind it are essential for developing educational insight among teachers. The knowledge of various components of senior secondary education in the academic stream will enable them to understand its nature, purpose, philosophy and problems. They will be aware of the curriculum, pedagogy and evaluation techniques relevant to this stage and acquire the knowledge of psychology of teaching, learning and transacting the curriculum and the action research to solve day-to-day problems. Teachers will acquire knowledge of the methods of teaching in depth and develop related competencies by means of the specialised programmes.

Practical work, the pedagogical analysis of the subject and practice teaching in the class under the supervision of the expert will inculcate among them needed competencies. The related practical activities like action research, field work, project work and sessional and practical work will develop problem-solving approach.

The preparation and use of instructional technology will make them more effective in the classroom. The preparation and administration of teacher-made objective tests will transform their approach to evaluation. They will be able to guide the students how to use library and laboratory for independent studies. The theoretical and the practical components mentioned in this curriculum frame will, thus make them competent and reflective teachers.

Transacting Curriculum

For the purpose of transaction a course may be divided into units and then modular approach may be followed. Pupil teachers may be encouraged to pursue independent and group studies. Seminars and workshops may be arranged. Lectures should only be indicative. The teacher may start the lecture analytically and through interactive interventions arrive at synthesis at the end. The skills of listening, drawing conclusion, conceptualisation, and identifying the central theme and its relevance to life be established. After each lesson, reference materials may be suggested. The main thrust of transactional modality will be on the development of abstract, critical and creative thinking alongwith inculcation of habit of precision and comparison and use of appropriate words and concepts.

Pedagogical analysis should precede the actual teaching. The notes of lesson may be only indicative. Its centrality should be focussed on the realisation of objectives. Supervision shall be the joint responsibility of the school and training colleges. At least three fourth of the lessons will be supervised by the expert in detail. Its nature should be formative. The projects shall be completed under the guidance of an expert and sessional/practical work shall be properly planned. The organisation of the student and physical education activities and services will be supervised by teacher educators.

Multiple approach will be adopted for the purpose of evaluating achievement for the theoretical content. It will be continuous as well as annual, internal as well as external. Teacher-made objective type of tests, diagnostic and prognastic tests, etc. shall be used for the purpose. The essay-type question will also be used for identifying abilities not detected by other tests. Continuous progress record of the students maintained by the teacher will be considered at the time of evaluation of the practice of teaching. The different kinds of practical work, project report, sessional work, tests and records of various activities shall be evaluated by experts in the area internally and continuously for giving proper feedback.

The evaluation strategy at this stage shall aim at identifying the students' potentialities teaching at the senior secondary stage.

A separate B.Ed. programme as envisaged in the framework may be organised by colleges of education and university departments of education. The teachers who have undergone a B.Ed. course for secondary stage and Master's degree in any of the academic subjects may subsequently undergo a bridge course or earn additional credits needed for developing competencies relevant to this stage under a specially designed programme of suitable duration.

Vocational Stream

The focus of vocational courses is on self-employment or employment which demand different capabilities, competencies and practical and academic skills from the teachers. The teachers of vocational subjects should not only possess high competency in a trade or vocation but also be able to enthuse their students to undertake it as a career and develop qualities essential for achieving success in this area. The preparation of teachers for teaching vocational subjects, therefore, becomes an important function of teacher education programme at this stage.

The suggested curriculum with all its theoretical and practical components will develop among the teachers of vocational subjects knowledge, skills and competencies needed for a teacher of this stream. The teacher will not remain a narrow technician but possess a broader educational outlook. The success of vocational education depends on obtaining practical skills and competencies on which enough emphasis has been laid. The apprenticeship programme, on-the-job training and workshop practices have been given due importance.

Teachers will be able to teach elementary financial management, advertising, conducting market survey and project formulation for starting a vocation. They will also acquire knowledge about management, entrepreneurship and organisational behaviour with reference to a vocation. All these will make them competent teachers of vocational subjects.

Transacting Curriculum

Curriculum transaction will highlight the applicational aspect of theory to actual practice. Demonstration shall be one of its techniques. Practice of teaching shall be arranged in actual work situation by means of apprenticeship. Laboratory and workshop will be fully utilised. Projects will contain all the details. The evaluation of theoretical component will be done as in the academic stream. But the practice of teaching and practical activities will be performance-oriented. Both process and the product will be evaluated. The workshop practices and work done during apprenticeship will be evaluated and the quality of the product will be judged jointly by the teacher educator and technical expert. This programme is for the education of teachers who have already acquired degree or diploma in a vocation or trade. In case of teachers who have no such previous training an alternative programme of increased duration may be designed. An alternative and more effective programme of teacher preparation for vocational education may be a 4 or 5 year integrated programme.

TASKS OF PRE-SERVICE EDUCATION

Teacher education, with a view to making it relevant to the school system as well as training needs for preparing teachers at different levels will have to be further restructured, reorganised, and revamped. Multiple models of teacher education may have to be evolved by the universities and other agencies including National Council for Teacher Education. The innovative models to be undertaken have to be relevant from the point of view of the teacher educator as well as those who will assume the role of a professional, requiring interdisplinarity, broader vision and goal consciousness and commitment. These would lead to the improvement in the standards of teacher education and develop professional competencies. Another significant feature of such models would be their feasible and cost effective. The detailed course outlines will be developed by the universities through their various academic bodies. It, however, pre-supposes that the duration is suitably adjusted with the entry qualifications.

There are several workable propositions for evolving a variety of models like school based model, community based model, discipline-oriented models, integrated models, comprehensive models etc. Needless to say, it would be necessary to initiate integrated and comprehensive programmes of teacher preparation in both academic and vocational streams. The stage-specific and need-specific models will have to be evolved. These innovative models should be promoted and financially supported.

There has been a strong demand from a large section of teacher educators and educationists to increase the duration of B.Ed. course from one year to two years. However, change-over from one year to two years duration may require two-three years preparatory time. It is, therefore, recommended that the two year B.Ed. courses may be instituted after careful planning, development of detailed curriculum, suitable augmentation of infrastructure and necessary orientation of teacher educators, during the next two/three years. During the interregnum, the general teacher education programmes may be offered.

4

IN-SERVICE TEACHER TRAINING

Teacher education is a continuous process and its pre-service and in-service components are inseparable. Professional development of teachers begins with pre-service and gets renewed through in-service programmes. It, however, does not mean that there is a simple linearity between the two. There are elements of 'change' and 'continuity' in teacher education system which necessitate renewal and upgradation of skills and competencies. The in-service programmes are also organised to sustain the 'survival competencies' which the teachers acquired years ago, during pre-service education.

In the professional updating of teachers, changes in the societal goals, educational structure, curriculum framework, transactional strategies, evaluation techniques and management processes play a significant role. New advances emerging on the educational horizon have to be addressed to and teachers made aware of the same as well. Teacher development is a complex process. Teachers update themselves by putting in various efforts of self-learning, peer learning and interactions with the community. Other alternatives to professional development are participation in recurrent programmes, extension activities and continuing education programmes.

In-service teacher education programmes are essential in view of obsolescence as well as explosion of knowledge and are necessitated on account of changes in educational and social realities. Whenever teachers are required to execute new and different roles or get promoted to a position that requires new set of competencies, participation in appropriately designed in-service programmes is called for.

Advances in the fields of curriculum, evaluation, audio-visual aids, telecommunication, etc. demand updating and orientation of teachers. Innovations both at macro and micro levels, would fail if teachers are not equipped and properly oriented to implement. In the Indian context, the developments, such as the 10+2+3 pattern, the making of science compulsory upto class X, new practices in evaluation like internal assessment, question banks, continuous and comprehensive evaluation, scaling and grading, introduction of new areas like environmental education, population education, computer education, AIDS education, gender sensitivity, etc. demand in-service training of teachers.

In-service training programmes are offered in various ways. Resource institutions at the national level offer orientation programmes of varying duration for different target groups. Besides this modality there are others like attachments, visits, national exchange programmes and international study visits; which form a significant component of in-service programmes.

Pre-service and initial teacher education is reinforced by self-initiated learning, in-service teacher education programmes and recurrent and continuing education. Self-initiated learning involves study on one's own for professional development. Recurrent and continuing programmes are organised through seminars, workshops, orientation courses etc. as per the professional requirements.

In the changing context of globalisation, liberalisation and advances in tele-communication, teachers and teacher educators need to become conversant with international trends, internationalism, multi-culturalism, multi-racialism and other pluralities. Both pre-service and in-service teacher education programmes should be receptive to new thinking and new changes. However, reforms and innovations in education can reach schools in large magnitude and expeditiously through in-service education programmes.

FUNCTIONS OF IN-SERVICE TEACHER EDUCATION

In-service teacher education broadly perform the following functions:

- — updates teachers in issues concerning content, methodology and evaluation,
- — upgrades serving teachers in tasks with which they are currently occupied,
- — initiates and orients teachers to new roles and technologies,
- — provides opportunities for unqualified or underqualified on-the-job teachers to update and upgrade their knowledge.

While content, design and duration of each programme would be determined by one or more functions identified above, long range efficacy of any programme would also be judged by its impact on the following:

- — personality of the trainees;
- — motivation and commitment in matters relating to professional and self growth;
- — awareness of social realities; and
- — communication and evaluative skills;

OBJECTIVES OF IN-SERVICE TEACHER EDUCATION

In-service teacher education has to be organised for achieving the following broad objectives:

- — to upgrade the qualifications of under-qualified and/or untrained on-the-job teachers.
- — to upgrade the professional competence of serving teachers.
- — to prepare teachers for new roles.
- — to provide knowledge and skills relating to emerging curricular changes—content, process and evaluation.
- — to make teachers aware of critical areas and issues, like, competency-based learning, multigrade, multi-level and multi-channel teaching, teaching students of disadvantaged groups, meeting educational needs of children with learning problems, developing inquiry skills, use of mass media in education, community participation and educational development of dyslexic children.
- — to overcome gaps and deficiencies of pre-service education.

In-service programmes need to be built around 'transformational objectives', i.e. increasing motivational level, enriching self-concept, building climate of inquiry and making teachers reflective practitioners. The thrust of transformational objectives is to develop such qualities in teachers as would enable them to become receptive, perceptive, reflective, innovative and dynamic.

STRATEGIES OF IN-SERVICE PROGRAMMES

Strategies adopted in in-service teacher education programmes would vary programme-wise and theme-wise. One has to judiciously select an appropriate training strategy or a mix of training strategies keeping in view the theme, programme duration, background of participants, availability of resource persons, support material and technologies of training at hand. Training strategies would range from lecture-cum-discussion to project work, library work, group interaction, field visits.

Models of In-service Training

There may be many models of in-service training. Some of these are given below:

Face-to-face Institutional Model

In this model, the training institution offers in-service training programme on its premises using direct face to face training approach. It is most effective when the number of participants is around 30 to 40. Besides lecture-cum-discussion mode many other transactional strategies are also used namely project method, case method, library work, peer learning sessions, buzz sessions, and small group techniques. The merit of this approach is that there is a direct and sustained interaction between participants and resource persons. The limitation of this approach is that it cannot be used when the institution wants to train a very large number of participants within a short time.

Cascade Model

In this model number of persons to be trained is very large and training design is built on two or three tier systems. In the first level the key resource persons are given training. They train resource persons who in turn train teachers. The advantage of this model is that a large number of teachers can be trained within a short duration of time. However, it has its limitations. Knowledge and information passed on at the first tier of key resource persons and then at the second tier of resource persons get somewhat diluted resulting into transmission loss of training effectiveness.

Media Based Distance Education Model

With the advent of satellite technology and computers many training programmes are imparted using electronic media. Audio-conferencing and tele-conferencing are already being used. In these the electronic media play the key role and print material play a supportive role. The advantage of this model is that training objectives can be achieved within limited time period. The constraint of this approach is the limited availability of the technology itself, and its high initial investment.

EFFECTIVENESS OF AN IN-SERVICE PROGRAMME

Besides the above three models, some other important considerations contribute to effectiveness of an in-service training programme.

Locale

Training institutions at the national, state and district level organise training programmes generally at their respective institutions. These institution based trainings have their own strengths in terms of availability of resources. Their limitations are that they dislodge participants from their work place. This approach is often known as off-site approach. On the other hand using on-site approach many institutions organise training programmes at the school site itself. Thus participants are not dislodged from their work place. Extension programmes and on-site programmes take training to the doorsteps of schools/institutions.

Target Groups

At present in-service programmes are organised largely for teachers. A few programmes are also organised for headmasters, principals and other supervisory staff. This net has to be widened and many more categories of personnel brought into the fold. In-service teacher education programmes ought to be offered to all teachers working at pre-primary, primary, elementary, secondary and senior secondary levels. These could cater to teachers working in formal schools, non-formal centres, open and distance teaching institutions and institutions of physical education, adult education, special education, etc.

Teacher educators, in general, have limited exposure to in-service education. There is a need to train teacher educators at all levels. In fact, an apex institution needs to be set up for training of teacher educators. Alternatively some selected institutions may develop special expertise in training of teacher educators. Such institutions would have to develop relevant support material and undertake critical research studies relevant to in-service programmes of teacher educators. Besides teachers, supervisors and administrators, there are other categories like Zila Pramukh, Pradhan, Sarpanch etc. connected with Panchayat Raj System who have the responsibility to look after primary level education. Depending upon the resources available staff of the support system, including librarians, hostel wardens, etc. should also be exposed to various programmes to enhance their professional competence.

Transactional Strategies

An effective in-service education and training programme would use various transactional strategies like case study method, brain storming sessions, panel discussions, seminars, symposia, small group techniques, project work, library work and lecture-cum-discussion sessions. The organisers and the resource persons can make an in-service teacher education programme more effective and interesting if the age, experience and background of participants are appropriately used at the planning phase. Since in-service participants bring a lot of experience and way of looking at educational events, they can significantly contribute to the design and development of programmes.

Content

Content of in-service programmes would depend upon objectives of each programme which could be grouped under the following major categories:

— school subjects.

— pedagogy and methodology.

— emerging issues.

— teacher's new role.

The focus of in-service programmes is on developing competencies and commitments. The overall aim of in-service programmes is to enable teachers to improve their classroom activities, out-of-the-classroom activities, school activities and community activities.

Evaluation and Follow-up

Evaluation is a weak link in many in-service training programmes. In most of the cases in-service programmes are evaluated, if at all, on an ad hoc basis. Each in-service teacher education programme should have monitoring as an integral component so that effectiveness of a programme can be properly assessed and apraised. Programme evaluation should assess whether the required inputs were provided to the programme on time, the logistics properly looked after and coordinated, the reading materials provided to participants etc. Another aspect of programme evaluation should be to assess the gains of each participant. The other subtle aspect is the impact evaluation to assess the impact of the programme at the grassroot level and in the field situation.

Education and training programmes become more productive and effective when programme planning is participative and transactional strategies are interactive. The need of all in-service teacher education programmes must emerge from the grassroots. For example, under the centrally sponsored teacher education programme, District Institutes of Education and Training are expected to organise programmes for teachers in such a way that every elementary teacher gets a chance to participate in the programme of his or her choice at least once every five years. In this venture state level coordinating agency like SCERT can play a faciliative and co-ordinating role to ensure that need based in service programmes are launched.

5

TEACHER TRAINING FOR ALTERNATIVE SYSTEMS

Teachers are the torch bearers in creating social cohesion, national integration and a learning society. They not only disseminate knowledge but also create and generate new knowledge. They are responsible for acculturating role of education. The educational expansion, universalisation of elementary education, vocationalisation of secondary education, higher and professional education and overall quality of education are major challenges before the country.

The upsurge for universal education, expectation for better quality of life have led to the exploration of alternatives to formal system which suffers from inherent inadequacies of rigidity and structural deficiencies. These alternatives include non-formal education, adult education, distance education, and so on. While a good deal of work has been undertaken to spread and improve education through various alternatives, a major problem has been lack of trained functionaries. However, these functionaries cannot be prepared on the formal models of teacher preparation. Since they are required to perform functions of different nature, their training has essentially to be job-specific. Developing skills, competencies and commitments in the personnel involved in alternative strategies demand preparation and use of teaching and learning materials to be specifically designed for the programmes.

TRAINING TEACHERS FOR NON-FORMAL EDUCATION

Non-formal education consists of an organised sytematic and planned educational activity, essentially characterised by inbuilt flexibility and carried on outside the framework of the formal system. It provides learning experiences to children in the age group of 6-14 years who are not able to avail of the facilities of formal schooling. Children from the non-formal system are eligible to appear in the examinations leading to certification to join the formal stream.

In certain respects formal and non-formal education are similar as both are organised to augment, promote and facilitate learning. They differ in their institutional management and the organisation of the course content. The training of the functionaries at different levels including instructors, supervisors, material writers, project officers and managers is significant. The objectives of the training of the functionaries may be the following:

— to familiarise the functionaries with the latest developments in knowledge and technology specific to their job performance.

— to develop among them critical awareness about India's social reality.

— to acquaint them with special requirements of the groups they have to deal with.

— to provide them knowledge and skills as may help in the socio-cultural development of the clientele.

— to enable them to draw support from a wide variety of sources.

— to develop among them positive attitudes towards the under-privileged sections of society.

— to promote among them the desire to actively participate in the developmental activities.

Content of Course

The curriculum for the functionaries of the non-formal education would be need-based and job-specific, depending on the nature of the task they have to perform. However, there are certain essentials which need to be considered. These include:

— a sound background in India's composite culture, its unity and diversity

— science as an element of thought, its role in history and its impact on society.

— Indian National Movement and Constitution of India

— economic planning in India and its impact on economy and society.

— national development problems and issues.

— educational development and systems of contemporary Indian education

— environmental and population related issues.

— basics of human psychology and behaviour.

— communication skills, use of media and educational technology.

— production of instructional materials

— Identification of learners' needs and community interaction.

— practical / field work

Transactional Modalities

- organisation of induction and recurrent orientation programme of suitable duration.
- organisation of refresher courses and orientation programmes in the method and content.
- utilisation of community resources—human and material
- summer schools and short term training programmes.
- seminars, symposia and workshops
- interaction with local experts and skilled persons.
- use of supplementary educational devices, media and educational technology.
- evaluation.

Methods and Approaches

- Non-formal education may be included as an optional/compulsory course in all teacher education programmes and also in courses like MA (Education), MA (Community Development), MA (Social Work), MA (Rural Economics), etc.
- Resource persons may include principals and school teachers, teacher educators, experts from different academic disciplines and administration and social activitists.
- Participation of Non-Governmental Organisations and voluntary agencies may be encouraged in implementation of the programme.

TRAINING TEACHERS FOR ADULT EDUCATION

Adult education is expected to provide the skills needed to survive in the modern world for leading an effective and 'good life'. It includes adults of all ages. National literacy programmes focus specifically on those in the age group of 15-35 years in Indian context. It aims at developing the capacity of 'learning to learn' with or without the help of adult educator. Adult education concerns those who are not full time learners and have not been exposed to formal education. The knowledge gained and skills developed from it are utilised in a variety of situations. Thus, it has become need-based.

The objectives of the training of the functionaries may include the following:

— to enable them to develop social awareness.

— to develop skills related to functional literacy programmes.

— to liberate adults from the bondage of prejudice, bias, ignorance, superstition etc.

— to prepare them for the participation in developmental activities.

— to develop among the learner the desire and potentialities of 'learning to learn'.

— to inspire the adult learner with the sense of patriotism, global consciousness and the will to live together.

— to promote among them a sense of national and social cohesion.

— to enable them to combine personal dignity with civic responsibility.

— to understand the learners and their needs.

— to develop awareness of human rights and legal literacy.

— to enable them to understand environmental and population concerns.

— to develop humanistic, moral and ethical values.

Training Programme

The programme should be participatory, flexible, relevant, diversified and need-based. It might include, among other things, the following :

- — Psychological and Sociological Principles of Adult Learning
- — Problems and Issues of Adult Education.
- — Indian Heritage
- — Freedom Movement, Indian Constitution, Administrative System of India including Panchayat Raj.
- — Contemporary India and the World.
- — Scientific and Technological Literacy.
- — Planning and Developmental Activities.
- — Economic and Social Problems.
- — Problems of women, minorities and the under-privileged sections of the society.
- — Acquaintance with approaches and methods of teaching adults.
- — Right to information, social activism and legal literacy.

Transactional Modalities

For the functionaries in this field it is essential to promote their capacity of 'learning to learn'. Lectures should, therefore, be reduced to the minimum and emphasis should be laid upon self-learning through techniques, like:

- — workshops, seminars, debates and discussions
- — tours and excursions
- — library work, laboratory work and actual experience of work situations

— basics of language learning
— organisation of refresher courses and orientation programmes.
— short term training programmes.
— extension lectures
— use of supplementary educational devices, media and educational technology.
— evaluation

Methods and Approaches

— adult education may be included as an optional/ compulsory course in all teacher education programmes and also in courses like MA (Education), MA (Community Development), MA (Social Work), MA (Rural Economics), etc.
— Resource Persons may include principals and school teachers, teacher educators, experts from different academic disciplines and administration and social activitists.
— Participation of Non-governmental Organisations and voluntary agencies may be encouraged in implementation of the programme.

TEACHER TRAINING FOR DISTANCE EDUCATION

Distance education implies the provision of educational opportunity at the place of learner from a distance by means of multiple media such as self-learning materials, audio-visual gadgets and short-term personal contact programmes. Information technology and cybernetics are simultaneously being utilised for upgrading the knowledge and skills. In order that learning through distance education mode becomes effective, the following categories of functionaries need special inputs of training for persons involved in:

— development and production of reading materials including assignments.

— organisation and conduct of personal contact programmes.

— production of radio, television and computer programmes.

— use of teaching aids and technological gadgets and tele-conferencing.

— academic counselling and resource persons manning regional/study centres.

Objectives of the training programme for distance teacher educators are as follows:

— to enable the distance educators to understand the nature and purpose of distance education.

— to develop among them the technique to prepare self-learning and self-instructional materials.

— to facilitate learning at one's own pace.

— to promote the habit of self-appraisal.

— to organise personal contact programmes.

— to identify and utilise learning resources.

— to enable them to establish a healthy linkage with the formal system and make distance education an effective means for the national and social development.

— to train them to make use of various interactive techniques.

— to enable them to prepare, utilise and evaluate the assignments.

PREPEARING TEACHERS FOR SPECIAL EDUCATION

Teachers with different skill levels are needed for special education programmes. Most of the general classroom teachers require sensitisation programmes whereas some teachers require specialised training to deal with severely disabled children.

The general training objectives in the area of special education are listed below:

— to create an awareness among all student teachers about education of children with special needs.

— to equip student teachers with skills to manage mild and moderately disabled children in general classrooms.

— to prepare resource teachers to serve specific categories of disabilities.

— to prepare multi-category resource teachers to serve more than one category of disability.

The general training objectives mentioned above will lead to the course objectives. These will vary between the levels of training like sensitisation, single category specialisation, multi-category specialisation. The course objectives may include the following:

— to understand the nature and causes of disability

— to acquire knowledge about the physiological and psycho-social implications of disability

— to understand the educational implications of various disabilities

— to develop positive attitudes towards students with disabilities

— to acquire skills to identify and assess levels of disabilities and provide appropriate educational services

— to apply the knowledge and skills acquired in the rehabilitation of students with disabilities

— to acquire competencies and skills to prepare and use relevant teaching-learning aids, technology and support materials.

— to develop skills in management of children with multiple disabilities

— to familiarise with education policies and programmes of the State and Central Governments regarding disabled children

— to understand practicalities of integrated education of disabled children

— to acquire techniques in educational assessment, evaluation and placement of disabled children

— to develop skills in encouraging family and community participation in rehabilitation of disabled.

Teachers for Disabled

For each category of impairment and disability special courses shall have to be designed to prepare specialised teachers. Products of such courses would qualify to work as resource teachers in general schools and general classroom teachers in special schools.

The curricular input for special teachers of disabled children may be as follows:

Theory

— Nature and characteristics of specific disability

— Social aspects of disability

— Medical aspects of disability

— Psychological aspects of disability

— Curriculum construction and adaptation

— Plus-curricular areas

— Methodology of Teaching
— Management of disabled children
— Special areas of concern: Student Activities and Physical Education
— Rehabilitation process
— Therapies

Practicum

— Observation of disabled children
— Practice teaching with appropriate adaptations for children with special needs
— Use of aids and appliances relevant to the area of specialisation
— Preparation of instructional materials
— Case study and project work
— Use of functional assessment procedures and identification of disabled children
— Visit to special education institutions and rehabilitation programmes
— Vocational modifications; removal of architectural barriers in access to playgrounds, dining hall, toilets, etc.

In-service programme is needed for all serving teachers to renew and upgrade their skills in dealing with children with special needs. In-service programme becomes imperative for the special education teachers to update themselves with the latest innovations and techniques of teaching in the field of special education. These would also apply to preparation of multi-category special teachers.

Teachers for the Gifted

In every society or school one can find children who are

much above the average and possess certain special abilities. They are referred to as the gifted or talented children. It has been observed that generally teachers are not properly trained to nurture the talent of such children. Every society needs the gifted and the talented for its progress. It is, therefore, necessary that proper provisions are made for their education.

In India certain schools have been started for the education of the gifted and the talented children. In these schools as well as in the general schools the teachers are appointed from the general pool of trained teachers whose training, by and large, is not oriented towards meeting the educational requirements of such children. Since giftedness and talent, like disability, have different shades and colours, the preparation of teachers should also be multi-dimensional.

Objectives of teacher education for the gifted in common school system are listed below:

- to develop among the prospective teachers the capacity to identify the special talent and the potentiality of the gifted and talented.
- to enable them to understand the psycho-social aspect of children.
- to develop among them the capacity to identify learners' needs and make suitable educational provisions.
- to empower them to evolve suitable curriculum, appropriate methods of instruction and evaluation and to promote self-learning.
- to enable them to promote proper socialisation among students.

To achieve the above objectives the following may be included in the general teacher education programmes.

— Giftedness—Meaning and Concept,
— Identification of the Gifted and the Talented,
— Methods of Nurturing the Talents of the Gifted,
— Continuous Monitoring,
— Case Study and Project Work.

PREPEARING TEACHERS FOR PHYSICAL EDUCATION

It is essential for the cultivation of vitality, courage, self-confidence, cooperativeness, leadership, obedience, discipline and positive attitude towards life and the world. The great educational thinkers like Plato, Rousseau, Gandhi, Aurobindo and Russell have laid great emphasis on it. Physical education stresses:

— development of sociability, obedience and discipline, acceptance of authority, positive attitude, equanimity, rapport with others and group consciousness.
— development of emotional stability, control over one's own feelings and temptations.
— development of mental health, ability to take immediate decision and prompt action.
— cultivation of the power of concentration.
— inculcation of democrative values.
— development of neuro-muscular skills
— formation of character and development of willpower.

Development of physical fitness and health of students is not the responsibility of the teachers of physical education alone. In fact, every teacher has a role to play in this direction, especially at the elementary stage and must have substantial exposure to physical education and health education. The teachers other than physical education teachers also need to take interest in games and sports and physical activities. Every prospective teacher irrespective of the level needs to be made conversant with the basics of physical education. In addition, every trainee is required to participate in at least one major group game and two items of sports. It needs to be provided for in the curriculum with a view to enabling them to generate a climate for promotion of physical activities.

Curriculum for Physical Education should be viewed from the following two angles:

- — Physical education as an integral part of teacher education programmes at all levels.
- — Physical education specifically for preparing teachers of physical education.

The objectives of physical education as an integral part of teacher education may be as follows:

- — to enable teachers to be conversant with the basics of physical education
- — to enable them to understand the relationship between general education and physical education
- — to enable them to organise games and sports and physical activities

The expected outcome of such an approach will lead to universalisation of physical education activities in schools.

Teachers of Physical Education at the Elementary Stage

These courses leading to a certificate or diploma are being suggested for the teachers of physical education at the elementary stage. The programme aims at realising the following objectives:

— to enable prospective teachers to understand the nature and purpose of physical education at elementary stage

— to develop among the students awareness of basic principles of health, hygiene and nutrition

— to enable them to develop good health and sound physique of students

— to foster interest in physical exercises, games and sports

— to inculcate the spirit of healthy competition and leadership

— to develop team spirit and fellow feeling

— to promote among them the competencies for organising different kinds of activities in physical education

— to enable them to develop among students the physical and mental alertness

— to enable them to develop emotional stability and self-control

Teachers of Physical Education at the Secondary Stage

B.P.Ed. programme is intended to prepare the teachers of physical education for the secondary schools. The programme aims at realising the following objectives:

— to enable teachers to understand the nature, purpose and philosophy of physical education at the secondary stage

— to prepare teachers of physical education with broader educational perspective

— to develop potentialities for planning and organising physical education programmes and activities

— to develop capacity to organise leisure and recreational activities

— to empower them to inspire their students to actively participate in physical and yogic exercises, games and sports

— to enable teachers to develop personality, character, will-power, democratic values and positive attitude towards life among their students

— to make teachers capable of imparting basic knowledge about health, hygiene and nutrition

— to develop skills and competencies to organise school and community games and sports

— to cultivate the spirit of sportsmanship, mental and physical alertness, scientific temper and optimism

— to promote mental health, power of self-decision and self-control, correct judgement and action, emotional stability and equanimity, respect for others and acceptance of authority and rules

— to promote appreciation and interest for indigenous games, sports and yogic exercises.

— to create awareness about health and hygiene in the community.

Masters Course in Physical Education (M.P.Ed.)

The Masters programme is intended to prepare teacher educators for physical education. Its objectives may be the following:

— to enable prospective teacher educators to understand the nature, purpose and philosophy of physical education

— to develop competencies necessary for physical training and coaching

— to develop knowledge, skills and competencies necessary for imparting physical education

— to enrich knowledge of personal and community health

— to promote the capacity to organise games, sports and recreational activities

— to provide knowledge of sports, medicine and physiotherapy

— to develop competence to undertake research in physical education, games and sports

— to enable them to prepare good athletes

— to inculcate the spirit of sportsmanship

— to foster interest in physical education and appreciate its role in school and society

— to prepare for evolving stage-specific curriculum, pedagogy and evaluation techniques in physical education

— to develop an understanding and appreciation of indigenous approach to physical education, exercises, games and sports.

6

ICTs IN TEACHER TRAINING

Educational systems around the world are under increasing pressure to use the new information and communication technologies (ICTs) to teach students the knowledge and skills they need in the 21st century. The 1998 UNESCO World Education Report, *Teachers and Teaching in a Changing World,* describes the radical implications ICTs have for conventional teaching and learning. It predicts the transformation of the teaching-learning process and the way teachers and learners gain access to knowledge and information. With the emerging new technologies, the teaching profession is evolving from an emphasis on teacher-centred, lecture-based instruction to studentcentred, interactive learning environments. Designing and implementing successful ICT-enabled teacher education programmes is the key to fundamental, wide-ranging educational reforms.

Teacher education institutions may either assume a leadership role in the transformation of education or be left behind in the swirl of rapid technological change. For education to reap the full benefits of ICTs in learning, it is essential that pre- and in-service teachers are able to effectively use these new tools for learning. Teacher education institutions and programmes must provide the leadership for pre- and in-service teachers and model the new pedagogies and tools for learning.

In many of the countries targeted with this curriculum, ICTs are in the early stages of development in commerce, industry, and particularly, in society. Communities and regions may have very limited resources, so it is important to undertake a careful analysis using an ethnographic approach to develop an organic strategy for the growth and development of education and teacher education that takes advantage of ICTs. The vision is not simply of ICTs, but of better education facilitated through the adoption and promotion of ICTs.

The Society for Information Technology and Teacher Education has identified basic principles for development of effective ICT teacher education. These are:

— *Technology should be infused into the entire teacher education programme*. Throughout their teacher education experience, students should learn about technology and how to incorporate it into their own teaching. Restricting technology experiences to a single course or to a single area of teacher education, such as methods courses, will not prepare students to be technology-using teachers. Pre-service teacher education students should learn about a wide range of educational technologies across their professional preparation, from introductory and foundations courses to student teaching and professional development experiences.

— *Technology should be introduced in context*. Teaching pre-service students basic computer literacy—the traditional operating system, word processor, spreadsheet, database, and telecommunications topics is not enough. As with any profession, there is a level of literacy beyond general computer literacy. This more specific or professional literacy involves learning to use technology to foster the educational growth of students. Professional literacy is best learned in context. Pre-service students should learn many uses of technology because they are integrated into their coursework and field experiences. They should see their professors and mentor teachers model innovative uses of technology; they should use it in their own learning, and they should explore creative uses of technology in their teaching. Teacher educators, content specialists, and mentor teachers should expose pre-service teachers to regular and pervasive modelling of technology and provide opportunities for them to teach with technology in K-12 classrooms.

— *Students should experience innovative technology-supported learning environments in their teacher education programme.* Technology can be used to support traditional forms of learning as well as to transform learning. A PowerPoint presentation, for example, can enhance a traditional lecture, but it does not necessarily transform the learning experience. On the other hand, using multimedia cases to teach topics that have previously been addressed through lectures may well be an example of a learning experience transformed by technology. Students should experience both types of uses of technology in their programme; however, the brightest promise of technology in education is as a support for new, innovative, and creative forms of teaching and learning.

While the proposed ICT in teacher education curriculum should aspire to no less, the trajectory of the development for countries, regions, and organisations should be appropriate to the level of resources, including expertise, leadership, and ICTs themselves. A widespread approach to reach a scattered population of teachers and organisations that are ready to move a small step forward with very limited resources may be helpful at an early stage. Creating centres of transferable excellent practice that encourage 'reference site' visits, and mentoring teachers in other locations, are also approaches that may be effective.

Approaches to the professional development of teachers must be dependent on context and culture. Since there are a variety of approaches, an overview of the many stages in which teachers receive teacher education may prove helpful. Professional development to incorporate ICTs into teaching and learning is an ongoing process and should not be thought of as one 'injection' of training. Teachers need to update their knowledge and skills as the school curriculum and technologies change. Individuals develop in stages and mature over time. Personal development must be accompanied by organisational development in schools, training centres, and universities.

In many regions, teachers engage in preparation before they start teaching in schools,this stage is referred as pre-service teacher education. When pre-service teachers begin to teach they may be given additional support to handle the complexity of their work for the first to third years of their career. This stage of professional development is called induction. The induction stage demands a great deal of effort and commitment, and research in developed countries reveals that around 30% of teachers may drop out during this time. Some teachers do not have the benefit of a preparatory course and must learn while teaching in schools, a condition referred to as on-the-job training. Such training is probably carried out within the school, perhaps with the teacher receiving some release from normal duties. Teacher education is an ongoing process of lifelong learning. The final stage, consisting of additional professional development, is called in-service teacher education.

It is important to note that some very strong models of teacher education provide simultaneous professional development for more than one group. For example, pre-service preparation can be aligned with in-service teacher education. A practising teacher may work with a pre-service teacher education student on an innovative educational project. This not only increases the research potential of the in-service teacher, but the pre-service teacher also experiences role modelling and, as a result, may have an easier transition into teaching. Professional learning communities allow teachers to support the professional development of colleagues and receive support themselves.

ICTs have increased the access to and reach of such professional associations. Mentorship can be fostered across geographic distances and supported by synchronous and asynchronous interaction. Professional development may also be enhanced by public or private partnerships with the community. Such partnerships may be particularly appropriate for professional development related to ICTs, with financial and technical support contributed by ICT companies, such as the Intel Teach to the Future Programme, or by local communities.

The professional development of teacher educators is also essential. Unless teacher educators model effective use of technology in their own classes, it will not be possible to prepare a new generation of teachers who effectively use the new tools for learning. It is also important to consider the question of who may teach. With ICTs, students often become teachers, using the processes of peer tutoring or reciprocal mentoring. Indeed, a teacher may facilitate learning by reversing the teaching-learning roles, with students acting as expert learners who model the learning process. ICTs provide extensive opportunities for this to occur in ways that can increase the self-esteem, motivation, and engagement of students.

Teachers need encouragement to adopt such strategies rather than to feel ashamed to be taught by young learners. Members of the community also may become teachers, or at least invited experts. ICTs extend the range of such opportunities and provide access to extensive relevant supporting materials. The teacher's role changes to manager and facilitator in many of these situations as the teacher helps the expert communicate with the learners and scaffolds the learning process. The teacher also acquires professional development by learning from the expert. The focus of professional development should also be expanded to those who work with teachers: the classroom assistants, school leaders, and members of regional and national organisations for curriculum and professional development. A common vision for the role of ICTs in education is important for its success. Teachers may find it impossible to incorporate ICTs into their work without support and encouragement from colleagues, parents, and leaders.

ICTs AND TEACHER EDUCATION

The most obvious technique for professional development for teachers is to provide courses in basic ICTs knowledge and skills, delivered by experts in national and regional centres. These types of courses, taught at training centres or universities with a syllabus set by regional or national agencies, have been a common practice in many countries. However, this approach has had limited success without follow-on training and support, as compared to effective use of ICTs by trained teachers. Similarly, courses for teachers in particular software and hardware applications are difficult to implement in a way that results in use of these applications in classroom instruction or other professional practices without additional support. The development of ICTs does not improve education if the focus is on ICTs. The vision must focus on what ICTs can do to improve education.

Over the last decade, many countries that included ICTs in education were slow to also include it in teacher education. Only recently have national agencies begun to realise the importance of educating teachers at the beginning of their careers. Younger people are more likely to be familiar with ICTs, to be adaptable, and to not yet have formed habitual modes of instruction that are more difficult to change with more experienced teachers. It is in the pre-service stage that they are most open to learning how to infuse technology into instruction. Based on their long experiences with traditional modes of learning, teacher educators may find it challenging to incorporate ICTs into their own instructional practices. They may also lack experience in developing the complex partnerships between higher education and schools that facilitate technology-rich contexts for training student teachers. To bring this about, it is usually necessary that the faculty be held accountable to standards and that the institution provides both incentives and resources to support technology-rich programmes and initiatives.

One approach that encourages collaboration between the teacher preparation programme and the community is the formation of computer clubs for students interested in computers and education. This approach was used successfully in Russia and works well where computing resources are limited. Care must be taken, however to ensure that the emphasis is on education rather than on games or competitions. Peer tutoring models are very effective in club settings and may develop into reciprocal mentoring with teachers in which the students provide ICT training for peers and teachers and the teachers mentor the tutors' developing skills as teachers. Peer tutoring is a relatively common approach in classrooms of cultures around the world. This approach is effective even when teachers have little ICT skill and knowledge. Parents and other community members may also serve as teachers, tutors, and co-learners, and the whole community may benefit economically because of an increase in the ICT skills among diverse members of the community. GenY is a peer tutoring approach that has been successful in many places, including the Caribbean and the USA.

Teacher Training through ICTs

ICTs may also support effective professional development of teachers in to how to use ICTs. A limited initiative to integrate an innovative approach to teaching and learning with one new technology for a large population of teachers can be an important early step for a nationwide strategy. The UNESCO document, Teacher Education Through Distance Learning describes interactive radio, a professional development model in which radio programmes provide daily half-hour lessons introducing pupils to English through active learning experiences with native English speakers. The radio programmes reach 11,000 teachers across South Africa. The initiative is successful in developing teachers' pedagogical, language, and technology skills. Much of this success is due to the appropriateness of the technology choice for South Africa.

When ICTs are introduced into a community, they may address multiple goals and may expand our conception of education. For example, the Drik project in Bangladesh started as an ecology project. The goal was to plant trees and educate the local population in how to care for them. The project brought a single computer with an Internet link into the community. The introduction of this computer, coupled with peer tutoring, resulted in the development of considerable ICT skills in the young people of the region, and today the school is a centre for ICT services both locally and globally (including the USA). Although the teachers were not the leaders in this initiative, they learned to adopt ICTs and incorporate them into the curriculum and administration of their school. This extension of the 'business' of the school beyond traditional education tasks is not unusual for schools in economically depressed communities that learn the value of technology in enhancing vocational opportunities.

MirandaNet is an important example of teachers who use ICTs to mentor each other and to establish new communities connected through the Internet. The brainchild of an active teacher educator and consultant, MirandaNet is supported by partners in business and commerce. Originating in the UK, MirandaNet has spawned related communities in the Czech Republic and Chile, and negotiations are underway for a Chinese MirandaNet.

FRAMEWORK ICTS IN TEACHER EDUCATION

In planning for the infusion of ICTs into teacher preparation programmes, several factors important to a programme's success must be considered. This section provides a holistic framework to assist in designing the integration of ICTs into teacher education. The framework is coherent with the context provided by today's society and reflects more recent understandings of the nature of learning, including aspects of learning communities during the school years and beyond into lifelong learning. The holistic framework will help teacher educators and administrators consider the cultural and educational system context, technology resources, and other factors that are important in planning the integration of technology into the pre-service curriculum. Limited technology resources and conditions of rapid change in educational, economic and political systems challenge many contexts of this curriculum. In some regions, the shortage of teachers, teacher educators, facilities and standards has been chronic for years and has reached crisis proportions. Access to ICT resources may also be quite limited.

A generic ICT in teacher education curriculum framework is provided in Figure 1. The encompassing oval underscores that the framework should be interpreted as a whole. To select parts or to simply copy the framework in rote fashion without taking care to understand the synergy of the whole would be a mistake. As the term synergy implies, the whole is more than the sum of its parts. For example, an approach resulting from informed leadership and vision is essential for ensuring that all the components of planning and implementing a technology integration plan are present and that they support one another.

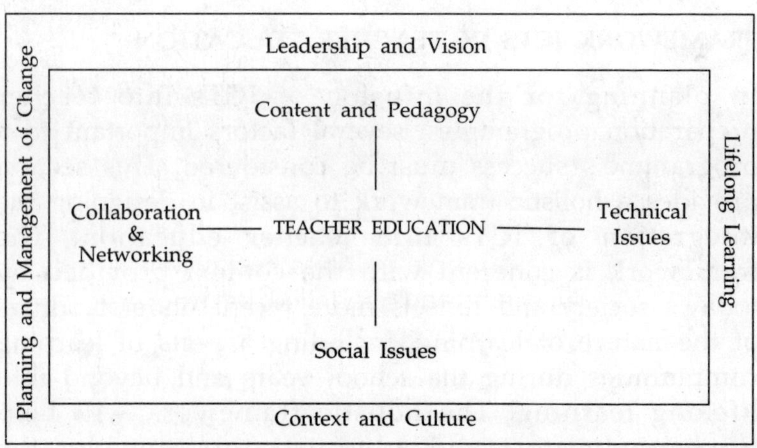

Figure 1. A Framework for ICTs in Teacher Education

The framework was designed by representatives of international projects to assist policy makers, course developers, teacher educators, and other professionals who are charged with developing the use of information and communication technologies (ICT) in teacher education. The model will help assure that national and local infrastructure, culture and context, among other factors, will be considered in designing new curricula, and that curricula will be kept up to date, as new developments are forged in education and ICTs.

Figure 1 shows the curriculum framework is comprised of four clusters of competencies encircled by four supportive themes. The curriculum framework also suggests that each teacher is allowed to interpret the framework within his or her context and personal approach to pedagogy, which is always related to the subject discipline or content area, rather than to the technology itself.

Themes that Bind Curriculum

The four themes that bind the curriculum as a whole are described briefly below:

1. *Context and Culture* identifies the culture and other contextual factors that must be considered in infusing technology into teacher education curriculum. It includes the use of technology in culturally appropriate ways and the development of respect for multiple cultures and contexts, which need to be taught and modelled by teachers.
2. *Leadership and Vision* are essential for the successful planning and implementation of technology into teacher education and require both leadership and support from the administration of the teacher education institution.

3. *Lifelong Learning* acknowledges that learning does not stop after school. In common with the other themes, it is important that teachers and teacher preparation faculty model lifelong learning as a key part of implementation, and as an ongoing commitment to ICTs in teacher education.
4. *Planning and Management of Change* is the final theme, born of today's context and accelerated by technology itself. It signifies the importance of careful planning and effective management of the change process.

These themes may be understood as a strategic combination of approaches that help teacher educators develop the four core competencies. The core competencies may be seen as clusters of objectives that are critical for successful use of ICTs as tools for learning.

Competencies

The ICT competencies are organised into four groups. *Pedagogy* is focused on teachers' instructional practices and knowledge of the curriculum and requires that they develop applications within their disciplines that make effective use of ICTs to support and extend teaching and learning. *Collaboration and Networking* acknowledges that the communicative potential of ICTs to extend learning beyond the classroom walls and the implications for teachers development of new knowledge and skills. Technology brings with it new rights and responsibilities, including equitable access to technology resources, care for individual health, and respect for intellectual property included within the *Social Issues* aspect of ICT competence. Finally, *Technical Issues* is an aspect of the Lifelong Learning theme through which teachers update skills with hardware and software as new generations of technology emerge. The following is a description of the four competencies.

Pedagogy

The most important aspect of infusing technology in the curriculum is pedagogy. When implementing the pedagogical competencies for infusing technology, the local context and the individual approach of the teacher linked with that of their subject discipline must be paramount. Teachers move through stages as they adopt ICTs. Initially, the teacher adopting technology applies it simply as a substitute for current teaching practice where technology is not used. The adaptation of ICTs by teachers should challenge and support changes in teaching practice, building upon individual pedagogic expertise.

As teachers' pedagogical practices with new technologies continue to develop, and organisational support and access to ICTs grow, it becomes possible to move beyond the adaptation of ICT applications that fit with existing practice. Transformation of the educational process will start to emerge and may move toward more student-centred learning environments.

In sum, as professional teachers educators continually develop their pedagogical use of ICTs to support learning, teaching, and curriculum development, including assessment of learners and the evaluation of teaching, they will:

— demonstrate understanding of the opportunities and implications of the uses of ICTs for learning and teaching in the curriculum context;

— plan, implement, and manage learning and teaching in open and flexible learning environments;

— assess and evaluate learning and teaching in open and flexible learning environments.

Collaboration and Networking

ICTs provide powerful new tools to support communication between learning groups and beyond classrooms. The teacher's role expands to that of a facilitator of collaboration and networking with local and global communities. The expansion of the learning community beyond the classroom also requires respect for diversity, including inter-cultural education, and equitable access to electronic learning resources. There is growing evidence that communities learn through collaborative activities that reflect diverse cultures in authentic projects that serve society.

Both local and global understandings can be enhanced using ICTs. The development of teachers' competencies in networking and collaboration are therefore essential to ICTs in education. Through collaboration and networking, professional teachers promote democratic learning within the classroom and draw upon expertise both locally and globally. In this process, they will:

- — demonstrate a critical understanding of the added value of learning networks and collaboration within and between communities and countries;
- — participate effectively in open and flexible learning environments as a learner and as a teacher;
- — create or develop learning networks that bring added value to the education profession and society (locally and globally); and
- — widen access and provide learning opportunities to all diverse members of the community, including those with special needs.

Social Issues

The power to access information and communication technologies brings increased responsibilities for everyone. Legal and moral codes need to be extended to respect the intellectual property of freely accessible information. Copyright applies to web resources, too, regardless of the ability of the user to purchase the rights. This respect can be modelled in classroom practice with students from an early stage. The challenges faced by society, locally and globally, by adoption of technology should become part of the curriculum in a way that involves learners and helps them to develop an effective voice in the debates.

Health issues of ICTs also need to be addressed. For example, prolonged engagement with ICTs requires appropriate support for the body, especially the hands and back. Similarly, hazards of electricity and other power sources require care and the modelling of safe practice. The technology standards for students and teachers from the International Society for Technology in Education (ISTE) offer guidelines for social issues, under the topic of social, ethical, legal, and human guidelines relating to the responsible use of technology.

In sum, professional teachers need to understand social and health issues surrounding ICTs and apply that understanding in their practice. Specifically, they need to:

— understand and apply the legal and moral codes of practice, including copyright and respect for intellectual property;

— reflect upon and lead discussion of the impact of new technology on society, locally and globally; and

— plan and promote healthy use of ICTs, including seating, light, sound, and related energy sources.

Technical Issues

Technical issues regarding integration of ICTs into the

curriculum include the technical competencies and provision of both technical infrastructure and technical support for technology use throughout the curriculum. Technical competencies of the individual are perhaps the most obvious but perhaps the least important in the long-term because use of technology should ultimately become transparent.

When technology is robust and used competently, it moves from the foreground to the background and remains essential. This is similar to the process of gaining any new skillset, such as riding a bicycle. Each new skill must be consciously attended to and practiced until it becomes an automatic response. Competent bike riders do not focus on balance and the pedals of the bike, they focus on navigation and safety.

However, we do recognise that in many contexts, the lack of technology competence, infrastructure, and technical support can create barriers to access and reliability resulting in diminished support for the curriculum. Additional technical support or training is therefore advised, depending on local circumstances.

Simply providing the technology for learners and teachers is not enough. The type and level of access is also important. ICTs will improve learning very little if teachers and students have only rare and occasional access to the tools for learning. Reasonable access to ICTs has been shown to be important for the acquisition of competence with hardware and software, especially for teachers. For example, provision of portable computers is an important strategy for ICTs teacher education. Teachers with portable computers can use them for both teaching in school and for other professional activities elsewhere.

In sum, professional teachers, provided with reliable technology infrastructure and technical assistance, demonstrate continual growth in their skill with ICTs and knowledge of their current and emerging applications within education and local and global society. Specifically they are able to:

- use and select from a range of ICT resources to enhance personal and professional effectiveness; and
- willingly update skills and knowledge in the light of new developments.

STRATEGIES FOR INTEGRATING ICTS INTO TEACHING

In an effort to implement ICT standards in a variety of coursework taken by preservice teachers across all subject disciplines, a number of methods and strategies have been identified. Many of these strategies employ commonly used productivity tools such as word processing, database, spreadsheet, or browser applications. These software tools can be used in countless ways to support the subject area curricula.

Web-Based Lessons

WebQuests

A WebQuest is an inquiry-oriented activity in which most or all of the information used by learners is drawn from the Web. WebQuests are designed to use learners' time well, to focus on using information rather than looking for it, and to support learners' thinking at the levels of analysis, synthesis, and evaluation. The WebQuest model (Table 1) has been effectively applied to all levels of education, from elementary to postgraduate study, and in many different subject Areas. The WebQuest provides teachers an option of reviewing and selecting web-based learning activities in a lesson type format.

Table 1. WebQuest Lesson Format

Introduction:	Orients the learner to what is coming and creates interest in the lesson
Task:	Describes what the learner should have completed at the end of the exercise
Process:	Describes the steps the learner should go through in completing the task
Resources:	Gives a list of Web pages the instructor has located that will help the learner accomplish the task
Evaluation:	Provides a rubric for examining six aspects of the student product
Conclusions:	Presents an opportunity to summarize and reflect upon the experience, examines the process, generalizes what was learned.

The WebQuest model encourages teachers to create for their students new activities and adapt successful ones to take advantage of the Web's power. A higher-level application of this model has students develop their own Web-Quest activities to support the subject matter they are studying, and share the WebQuests with their peers.

CyberGuides

CyberGuides include standards-based, web-delivered units of instruction centred on core works of literature. CyberGuides provide a quick supplementary set of activities for students (and pre-service teachers) as they explore specific pieces of literature. Each CyberGuide contains a student and teacher edition, targeted standards, a description of the task, a process by which the task may be completed, teacher-selected web sites, and an assessment rubric. The teacher's guide includes an overview of the activities, suggestions from the author, and a library of links. The student guides include activity directions written in a format appropriate for the age and reading ability of the students.

Multimedia Presentations

Multimedia combines media objects such as text, graphics, video, animation, and sound to represent and convey information. In this project-based method of teaching and learning, students acquire new knowledge and skills by designing, planning, and producing a multimedia product.

Many teachers find that students are motivated to learn when they can use technology to present the results of a rich project or activity. The multimedia presentation contains content conveyed by the student's selection of media. The teachers in training can look at examples of projects and lessons, at Internet sites housing collections of student samples. Some examples of multimedia presentations include:

- — creating a web page or site;
- — developing a branching hypermedia stack;
- — using a multimedia slide show application to create a computer presentation;
- — shooting and editing video to create a computer-generated movie.

As new forms of multimedia are explored, the types of projects become more complex. Multimedia-authoring tools are used to link and branch screens, making them interactive and layered with information in photos, scanned images, movies, and text. Students and candidates can easily narrate their projects using a microphone.

Telecomputing Projects

Telecomputing projects are Internet-enriched learning activities that often involve students in one location collaborating with students or adults in one or more other locations. They may share, among other things:

— experiences
— beliefs
— data
— information
— problem-solving strategies
— products they have developed or jointly developed.

Telecomputing tools include email, electronic mailing lists, electronic bulletin boards, discussion groups, web browsers, real-time chatting, and audio- and video-conferencing. Online resources include web sites, interactive environments, and remotely operated robotic devices.

Online Discussions

A common type of telecomputing activity is online discussion. With the growth of infrastructure around the world comes the ability to access others through remote connections. Students and teacher candidates can connect to experts and peers through a variety of formats, such as chat rooms, electronic bulletin boards, and email. Communicating online offers participants freedom to send and receive information efficiently across diverse geographic locations.

Communication can occur asynchronously allowing time for reflection, or to compensate for varying time zones. In real-time online communication, as in chat groups, the communication is synchronous and provides immediate feedback for reinforcement and understanding. Examples of online environments include email lists and virtual meeting places such as Tapped In. Tools such as Blackboard, and WebCT may be used to create online environments. Particular care should be taken when planning these activities across cultures and languages. Online discussions can provide rich learning experiences as the inter-cultural exchanges develop both linguistic skills and cultural knowl-edge. One successful strategy is for students to read in the target language, while writing in their native language.

The Three Pomegranate Network of Armenian provides an excellent example of connecting a society in Diaspora-almost two thirds of Armenians live outside their contemporary homeland. The project links different Armenian schools across the world, each with varying degrees of access to technology and training, but all wishing to strengthen their awareness of a shared personal heritage, including the Armenian language and alphabet.

The ICT curriculum for Armenian teachers is project-based and structured around a task, such as the production of a web-based newsletter. The project provides valuable strategies for the planning of curriculum across cultures and schools, which are summarised as follows:

— *Language*: Instructions and other input from the project designers are bilingual. Students work in the target language, Armenian in this case. Software has been developed to include the target language alphabet.

— *Points of contact*: Schools serving Armenian children are linked electronically to schools in Armenia in the collaborative projects. Home and community centres need careful development to act as coordinating centres for curriculum projects.

— *Informal catalyst*: An informal catalyst to collaboration is necessary. In this project, the school in Armenia always takes this role.

— *Community building*: the projects, exercise and games are specially designed for the Diaspora, including activities that introduce students new to their culture.

— *Connectivity*: The project uses a flexible set of connectivity solutions including: direct access, connectivity centres, the Web, and CD's as a means of providing wider access.

They further give guidance in setting up such a network, emphasising the important role of ICT teacher educators and leaders. There is a significant need for highly committed project managers to shepherd the project through its various stages. These stages include web and learning-activity design, identifying participants from a worldwide audience, and overcoming many logistical issues associated with adding content to a school curriculum and identifying Internet resources.

Projects such as this will be exhibited and supported through the Universal Forum of Cultures Education project. Applications to participate are available online. Guidance on the creation and support of virtual learning communities and information on potential partners may also be found in these and other web sites.

Quality Assurance

Quality assurance in teacher education is an ongoing process and is demonstrated in a number of different ways. The teacher education institution itself may be scrutinised along with individual programmes within the institution. The quality of the teacher education institution and its programmes is often judged by the performance of the teachers they produce and the success of their graduates in effecting improved student learning in their P-12 classrooms.

Quality assurance is often determined through an accreditation process. Demonstrated competence of teacher candidates in use of ICTs in teacher education has become increasingly important in making accreditation, certification, and programme review decisions. This is particularly true in the two countries that have adopted detailed national standards, the United States and the United Kingdom. Quality assurance is uncommon in other countries, except through the evaluation of projects and strategic initiatives.

ICTS AND TEACHERS' PROFESSIONAL DEVELOPMENT

The challenge confronting countries, regions and universities is to address the following basic principles for ICTs in teacher education:

— ICTs should be infused into the entire teacher education programme.

— Technology should be introduced in context.

— Students should experience innovative ICT-supported learning environments in their teacher education programme.

The most critical factor in the successful integration of ICTs into teacher education is the extent to which the teacher educators have the knowledge and skills for modelling the use of ICTs in their own teaching practices. To enable them to develop these skills requires a well-conceived and sustained programme of professional development.

Strategies

Countries that have initiated efforts to infuse ICTs into teacher education have found four professional development strategies helpful in successful technology integration. First, professional development needs to focus on teaching and learning rather than on hardware and software. It should be designed by first considering what student teachers are expected to know and be able to do in a specific discipline, and then infusing ICTs into the learning process so that acquiring the knowledge and skills is more efficient.

Second, professional development is practically useless unless leaders and teacher educators are provided with access to technology resources and have the time and support-when needed—to apply the new knowledge and skills that they have learned. A just-in-time approach to professional development is a model that works well. In this approach, professional development is provided to teacher educators when they have a need or opportunity to use a specific technology tool or application to enhance learning.

Third, professional development in the use of ICTs is not a one-time activity. To keep current with new developments means that professional development in ICTs must be an ongoing process.

A further strategy for professional development is to start in a small way. Start by providing professional development in the use of ICTs to a small group of teaching staff. Perhaps this group will have volunteered or demonstrated that they have basic ICT competencies for personal use, or have expressed personal interest in using ICTs in their teaching. Working with this small group allows the professional development staff to determine the specific interests and needs of the teacher educators and what works best in the professional development process. Based on this experience, professional development may be provided to other small groups of faculty, thus expanding and refining the professional development efforts.

The most important criterion for effective professional development is to tailor it to the learning needs and skill levels of individual teaching staff within a faculty. This suggests that, ideally, an institution should, based on availability of resources, provide a variety of options for professional development for the faculty. In structuring professional development options and resources, it is helpful to explore collaboration opportunities with partners outside the university. The opportunities for ICTs to create new paradigms of teaching and learning will depend largely on leadership and a shared vision, and on appropriate and continuing professional development.

The planning and implementation of ICT-related professional development of teacher educators should be led by a planning group that includes representation and expertise from teacher educators, programme administrators, teachers, school administrators, technology experts, and business leaders. The diverse perspectives of the group should provide an understanding of the realities of the classroom, new views of the teaching-learning process, knowledge of the array of technologies that may be used to enhance learning, and community opinions. It is important for a planning group to negotiate a shared understanding of the role of ICTs in the agenda for educational renewal based on their individual cares and concerns. It is also helpful to have a larger advisory or liaison group that may facilitate collaborative professional development efforts and sharing of resources across related organisations, for example, between the university and the partner schools where students are placed for teaching practice.

New Approaches to Teaching

An important aspect of professional development is not only enabling teacher educators to understand and use ICT tools in their teaching practices, but understanding how technology coupled with new approaches to teaching and learning, may enhance student learning. Many teacher educators recognise that approaches to education are changing and that new technology has the potential to improve education and student learning. They may also recognise the implications of increasing use of technology in society and employment, including employment directly related to their own disciplines and content areas. Less obvious are the implications for literacy and numeracy at the core of the educational process, and the need for teacher educators themselves to model good practice in their teaching so that their students can easily transfer these strategies into their own teaching practice. Teacher educators are experts in a domain, and it is important to respect this domain while helping them to revitalise and modernise their teaching with ICTs.

The most significant change required of individuals and organisations providing teacher education is to redefine student roles and responsibilities. This is referred to as student-centred learning, and in the context of teacher education means that control of the teachingleaning process must move away from the teacher educator to the student of teaching. Both students and teachers have always had rights and responsibilities, but the redefinition of the learning environment requires a change in the balance of rights and responsibilities, with the student assuming more of both. ICTs demand this shift because technologies are constantly changing. Students need to develop the ability to think for themselves, continually learn as technologies change, and provide support to one another. This last element, peer teaching, is a natural product of ICTs because often the younger generations bring increasingly high levels of competence into the learning environment. This is a positive shift, and it should be noted that these strategies (learning from peer support and reciprocal mentoring between teacher and learner) are also appropriate for competencies that do not involve ICTs.

Stages of Professional Development

Teachers and teacher educators develop ICT competence in stages. Those who are fluent with technology may not appreciate how difficult it is for technology novices to appropriate ICTs into their professional practice. Teacher educators often find this task even more difficult than teachers do, because they typically have higher levels of content and pedagogical expertise that must be respected. Teacher educators, because they have to work in multiple contexts—both the home institution and the field where students are placed to observe and practice teaching—may also be more influenced by the absence of the essential conditions for ICTs in teacher education.

Four stages are common, but they may be repeated with new forms of ICTs or applications of ICTs to new areas. The first stage for each individual is awareness, and the appropriate response at this stage is to provide information about a relevant application of ICTs and appropriate ways that it may be used in the individual's current professional or personal concerns. Please note the learner-centred nature of this approach; the concerns are not those of the supporter or the organisation, but of the individual teacher educator. Teacher educators then explore the use of the application. They need support to put this ICT application into practice in a timely manner and to reflect on its effectiveness. Only after teacher educators have gone through these stages are they able to adapt their practice to make better use of ICTs, and then move toward the final stage to become innovators and modellers of excellent practice for their students and colleagues.

The advent of ICTs provides the opportunity to engage in this process from a new perspective and to model processes of learning for colleagues and students. It is acceptable for teacher educators to adopt only those aspects of ICTs that are relevant to their practice, but they must first be allowed to explore the range of possibilities, so that they and their students may become critically aware of, and competent in, diverse ICT applications. Of course, any teacher educators continually strive to be responsive to developments and innovations in education within and beyond their discipline.

Case Studies

To understand the strategies of professional development it is important to understand how they are embedded in the broader context of the planning and implementation of ICTs in teacher education. The following paragraphs provides some case studies. These illustrate an eclectic range of strategies. Each case study is analysed by use of the framework for ICTs in teacher education.

Strategically Supported Workshops

A growing number of pre-service teacher education programmes in the USA have employed the ISTE technology standards, and ISTE describes the best of these programmes on the ISTE web site. One such programme was initiated at the University of Texas at Austin, where the teacher educators expert in ICTs have actively planned and promoted the professional development of their colleagues and facilitated the management of change. The culture is one in which all participants respect the leadership and vision provided by the dean and the college's technology support centre. The current programme evolved from the experiences gained in working with the teacher education faculty. It underscores the importance of learning from the mistakes, as well as the successes, in implementing professional development. For example, a faculty development workshop was held to teach faculty to use a tool to incorporate web-based elements into their teaching. An initial training session was offered that provided the faculty with an extensive demonstration of the full range of capabilities of the tool. The faculty participants left the two-hour session with cognitive overload and little that they could immediately apply to their courses.

Based on this experience, another workshop was designed that focused on a few useful applications that faculty could incorporate into their instruction. The teacher educators were asked to bring class syllabi and selected course resources to the workshop. The teacher educators learned how to post these materials online in WebCT and set up online class discussions. After the teacher educators had time to see how this worked in practice with their students, a second workshop was provided to help them consider appropriate ways to facilitate collaboration and networking, along with the social issues that might arise in using these methods. These redesigned workshops were highly successful and led to ongoing faculty development.

This effort was successful because this strategy permitted the teacher educators to gain new information about the software within a pedagogical approach that addressed their immediate concerns, and allowed them to pilot the approach and evaluate their efforts. A similar strategy works for other widely used software application tools, such as word processing and desktop publishing.

Reciprocal Mentoring

Successful models for professional development must

reflect this dynamic nature by building capacity rather than teaching skills. Reciprocal mentoring is an example of a professional development model that builds capacity within an organisation.

Iowa State University has an award-winning programme of teacher education and supports this excellence by providing professional development in ICTs for its teacher educators and the in-service teachers who work with students. Over a decade ago, the course Technology and Teacher Education was established to provide graduate students with an internship experience. Many of these students become teacher educators who are expert in ICTs. These students mentored teacher educators in ICT skills and, in return, the teacher educators mentored the students in their profession. The graduate students' advisor, who strategically selected or negotiated the participation of teacher educators, facilitated and planned the interaction. Over the years, the balance moved from encouragement of reluctant teacher educators to participate, to the strategic choice of participants from a long list of volunteers. Similarly, the context and culture became increasingly akin to a sociable family that supports one another; an organisation in which members learn from one another while collaborating and networking.

The mentoring course takes place in the fall semester. During weekly meetings, the graduate students learn about mentoring and a variety of approaches to infusing technology into education. These meetings foster collaboration and networking among the graduate students, lend moral support, provide opportunities for the development of technical skills, and engage students with relevant literature. Each student also meets with his or her teacher educator mentor weekly and responds to their needs at an appropriate pace.

In the early stages of this process, many teacher educators develop confidence with ICTs very slowly, often starting with word processing of scholarly work or with the creation of slides using software. Technical competence is purposefully developed slowly, to keep pace with the emerging confidence and autonomy levels of the teacher educator. The graduate students' advisor insists that mentoring graduate students assist the teacher educator to engage with ICTs, rather than allow the teacher educator to delegate the ICT tasks to the student mentor. ICT applications used in instruction are favoured over those for research, so that the mentoring graduate student can support and experience the development of pedagogic competence. The mentor pairs are expected to engage in many rich conversations as they work together, covering diverse themes and competencies, including social issues with ICTs and discipline specific topics.

Toward the end of the semester, the teacher educators join the mentors' class for a celebration of their collaborative professional and course development. At this time the teacher educators are exposed to a wide range of ICT applications, cultures, and contexts, and reflect on the four themes and competencies. The graduate students' advisor also reflects on the programme's success in reaching department and university goals and gains new ideas for future planning. This model has been extremely successful, as measured by increased faculty competence in the use of technology and by the attitudes of graduate students and faculty. It has been adapted to various settings, including those in which undergraduate students are the mentors.

International Technology Transfer

Occasionally opportunities for collaborative projects are stimulated by requests for technology transfer proposals.

This case study is of one such opportunity provided by the European Commission, which offered funding for faculty development to countries in Central and Eastern Europe.

The MATEN (Multimedia Applications for Telematic Educational Networks) project provided technical and pedagogical support to countries in Central and Eastern Europe. It researched ways in which information and communication technologies affect instructional design in this region and the ways existing patterns of social interaction in education are shaping the evolution of software engineering.

The project provided funding for infrastructure to universities in Ukraine, Lithuania, and Russia, and provided support to encourage retention of faculty and teachers in countries in transition. Because of the project, they were able "to expand the Flexible Distance Learning Systems (FDLS) model to describe possible applications of different multimedia in curriculum and courseware design". Two courses particularly relevant to this discussion are a course in ICTs for teachers in the former Soviet Union led by the Ukrainian Institute of Cybernetics in Kiev and a course at Kaunis University of Technology in Lithuania. The first stage of the course development took two years, followed by an additional contract to update and improve the courses with multimedia. This process set up the infrastructure and provided tailored ICT teacher education to the teacher educators who developed the first courses.

Rather than address the participants' stage of development, the project first took a more direct approach, with an assumption that content and technology could be simply linguistically translated for delivery. The participants, at an early stage in the professional development sequence, experienced more stress than success during these early days of the project.

The teacher educator participants had little experience of ICTs and were largely uninformed about recent pedagogical approaches, so their teaching tended to rely on textbooks and highly structured exercises. For this reason, a technology transfer course was created to enable the teacher educators to create a course suited to their own context and culture. A team developed the courses, and included teacher educators and ICT faculty from universities in these three countries as well as project staff.

This strategy permitted international experts to model appropriate pedagogic approaches, including collaboration and networking. The technology transfer course was built upon an English university's online ICT masters programme provided over the Internet for in-service teachers. This online learning environment was adapted over time in response to the needs of the target teacher educators. The teacher educators were helped to develop their own pedagogical skills, as they created content that placed ICTs into the context and culture of their region's schools and universities. The teachers who completed high quality work received a certificate from the English university. This certificate motivated them and provided one form of quality assurance.

Although distance learning formed the core of this project, the on-site ICT faculty provided their teacher educator colleagues with training to develop technical competence, and handled the technical issues as they arose. This support was essential to the teacher educators as they moved through the stages of development. The local ICT faculty also created course materials for technical aspects, which were used by the teacher educators for their courses. This project also illustrates the need to consider social issues when designing ICT professional development. There was difficulty in obtaining good access to ICTs for teacher educators due to their low status. This contributed to the stress they experienced as ICT novices and probably contributed to participant dropout. These and other social issues were sensitively handled by the project team as they arose. Other points identified in the framework under Social Issues did arise, including repeated attention to respect for copyright and intellectual property rights.

MATEN was a complex and ambitious project. Project staff provided vision and leadership and support for planning and the management of change. Dissemination activities carried out by the Ukrainian teacher educators spread the activities across the former Soviet Union and large numbers of teachers benefited from the course. These successes, although significant, could have been improved by making the process more transparent to those new to ICTs.

Enlaces Programme

Another example comes from Chile, a nation with many economic challenges that has used ICTs to accelerate educational reform. The national ICT initiative is called *Enlaces*. In common with all of the cited examples of good practice, the design was informed and led by ICT experts, and in this case, the team came from a leading university centre, the Instituto de Informatica Educativa of the Universidad de La Frontera. The centre conceived the initiative and has played a central role in the development of the *Enlaces* programme since 1993. In conjunction with the Ministry of Education, it is responsible for the national coordination of the *Enlaces* Educational Network. The Institute also conducts research and development activities to support the use of information and communication technology in the network's schools. The centre was informed by scholarly research in this area, and at least one of the ICT teacher educators undertook a doctoral degree on this topic with leading experts in the University of London Institute of Education. To inform early stages of development and ongoing evaluation the *Enlaces* initiative drew on a wide range of international consultants in ICTs in education, as well as this close doctoral level supervision.

The majority of ICT teacher educators in *Enlaces* were drawn from 24 universities, which became known as the Technical Assistance Network. This network was built upon a strategic alliance between the Ministry of Education and universities across the country. The Technical Assistance Network's mission was to train teachers and provide them with technical and educational support. Six universities, designated as Regional Centres, served as coordinators, managing *Enlaces* activities and teacher training in a particular geographical area of the country. They also carried out applied research in the field of educational ICTs. Eighteen universities, called Implementing Units, provided training within sub-zones under the supervision of a Regional Centre.

One of the fundamental premises of the Enlaces programme was that merely supplying information technology to schools is not enough to bring about significant changes in the quality of education. Although ICTs can potentially simplify and enhance the learning process in all subject areas and in some cases act as a catalyst for innovation, additional efforts such as teacher training and support must be done in order to produce sustainable changes in pedagogical practices and student learning outcomes.

The following principles guided the definition of overall strategies:

— Information and communication technologies are tools to be used by all participants in the educational process: students, teachers, school administrators, parents, and sponsors; thus, great emphasis was placed on teacher training and the development of a technical assistance network. The notions that learning computer skills is an end in itself and only experts can use ICTs were rejected.

— The goal is to not only equip schools with computers, but also to connect them with each other and the world through an educational network, thus enabling schools to exchange ideas and experiences regardless of their location. This goal also addresses one of the Chilean Educational Reform's key objectives: increasing equity in educational opportunity for all Chilean students.

— No single formula can be applied uniformly to all schools, and the uses to which computers and networks are put will depend upon each school's educational projects, needs, and social, cultural, and geographical environment.

These considerations, combined with the enthusiasm and initiative of teachers, administrators and students across the country, have often led to surprising results, with broader and deeper implications than those foreseen by the programme. *Enlaces* reached 100% of the secondary schools and 50% of the primary schools by 2000 (7 years), thus covering 90% of the school population. Within this group, *Enlaces* created an advanced group of ICT-using teachers in 51 schools from different areas of the country. The schools provided local reference sites to demonstrate ICT practice embedded in the local context and culture. *Enlaces* equipped these schools with more computers, technical support, and pedagogical assistance than the regular schools, with the expectation that they would become field-based ICT teacher education sites. As a result, these schools formed the core of the collaborative professional development activities that occurred through the Internet. The leading ICT teachers and teacher educators also received international collaborative support from the MirandaNet community of practice, as discussed in the case study.

The following were key strategic elements of the Enlaces plan to infuse ICTs into teacher education and throughout the educational system:

- *Teacher Training and Support*: The teacher training strategy in *Enlaces* includes three different initiatives:
  - Initial training over one year helps educators incorporate educational information technology into all aspects their teaching, with special training for one or more *Enlaces* coordinators per school.
  - Follow-up technical assistance allows the schools to continue the active incorporation of educational technology into their educational projects and to develop greater autonomy in this area.
  - Educational Information Technology Encounters encourage teachers to exchange experiences and to keep abreast of each other's practices. Students can observe the achievements of their peers in other schools, and the community gains a greater appreciation for the use of technological resources in its schools.
- *National Support Infrastructure*: The Technical Assistance Network was built upon a strategic alliance between the Ministry of Education and universities across the country, with a mission to train teachers and provide them technical and educational support. Twenty-four universities provided national coordinating centres to support six regional centres and eighteen implementation zones.

— *La Plaza: A Non-Intimidating Computer-User Interface:* La Plaza software was created to provide friendly access and a familiar interface to computers. The metaphor is a familiar market square where the images act as icons for each application. For example, clicking on the image of the post office gives access to electronic mail. The software was used to provide a non-intimidating first encounter with ICT technology. It was particularly successful in reducing teachers' anxiety toward a technology perceived as difficult.

— *Private Sector Support*: The development of the *Enlaces* network required support from the school communities themselves and from the private sector. Expanding the number of computer rooms, acquiring new educational software, servicing equipment, buying necessary supplies and providing Internet connections are ongoing challenges demanding hard work and commitment from the whole community.

Telephone companies in Chile donated telephone lines and unlimited Internet connections to the great majority of the country's primary and secondary schools. In addition, the companies provided free email accounts to all Chilean teachers and students. Numerous primary and secondary schools would not have been able to construct the computer rooms or upgrade computer infrastructure to join the *Enlaces* programme without donations from private companies and contributions from the school communities themselves.

— *Formative and Summative Evaluation*: The results of various evaluations of the *Enlaces* programme between 1993 and 1999 on the impact of ICTs on the educational system showed that there was

> growth in students' creativity, capacity for gaining knowledge about the world, and reading comprehension levels. Changes in learning levels in the area of mathematics could not be established.

Descriptive evaluation showed that ICTs sparked a high level of motivation among students, produced a more horizontal social organisation within the classroom, and made students feel proud of their participation in projects, with a corresponding increase in self-esteem. The evaluations also indicated an increase in teachers' managerial roles and improvements in the internal climate at schools. Furthermore, external evaluations showed that many of the teachers believed that communications via computers in their classes had improved the quality of the teaching-learning process. Two major challenges revealed by these evaluations are the need to supply schools with more computers and a greater variety of educational software, and the concern among teachers about their heavy unpaid workload.

The participating schools gained greater prestige in their communities, which translated into increases in enrolment (increased income via larger subsidies). School officials also valued the increase in equity that occurred as a result of the project's providing equipment that schools otherwise would not have been able to acquire and the country-wide spread of free access to Internet resources. The project also produced improvements in parents' perception of their schools' performances, which facilitates the learning and teaching process.

From a more global perspective, the evaluations made by the World Bank and the Agency for International Development praise the Enlaces project as one of the most successful programmes in Chile's efforts at educational reform. An important point in this positive evaluation is that the project has expanded its coverage to the national level without sacrificing quality or equity.

Among the factors in this success, the evaluations mention the programme's focus on teachers, the construction of a social network of educators and pupils facilitated by user-friendly technology and decentralised support, and respect for participating schools' autonomous decisions in the use of the programme's technologies. The evaluations also emphasise the high quality of the project's technical and administrative team, which has maintained a balanced mix of a clear vision, flexibility, and creativity in the face of new educational challenges and fast-changing technology.

An important conclusion that has emerged through observations of the schools is that innovation must arise out of current pedagogical practices. Teachers are more inclined to use technology if they can relate it simply and directly to their class work and to the materials and teaching models they use. To this end, *Enlaces* seeks to show teachers more clearly the multiple ways in which technology can be used, as much in the classroom as in extracurricular activities. The point is not to merely "do the same thing, only with computers," although in the beginning it may seem that way. The teacher invariably perceives changes in his or her class, at least in the organisation and motivation of the students. On the basis of these small initial changes and on clear evidence of the students' improved motivation, the teacher may try out more effective strategies or adapt those of other teachers.

Another interesting observation is that, due to the comprehensive initiative of the Chilean educational reform effort, computers are acting as catalysts for other initiatives that are not directly related to ICTs. Often, in the midst of many other programmes endeavouring to induce changes in a given school, it is the introduction of computers and telecommunications into the classroom that initiates change. This is not to say that computers by themselves are capable of causing innovation and change;

however, they certainly contribute in a substantial way to support the changes envisioned by other initiatives. The *Enlaces* programme continues to accept new challenges. Its achievements, combined with continuing advances in information and communications technology on a global level, have generated new goals for further expansion of educational information technology in Chile.

The project has adopted a modified cascade strategy to develop large numbers of ICT teacher educators. The central coordinating unit has led the development of workshops and materials to start the innovation, which is informed by their ongoing international research. The centre also leads soft-ware development and national negotiations to support the initiative. The regional centres modified these processes and materials to align with their contexts. They trained the teacher educators in the eighteen implementing units through workshops informed by wider teacher education activities. For example, staff conducted supportive visits to schools seeking the commitment of school leaders and an understanding of their educational objectives. Such visits proved particularly important in the early phases of the project. In late phases, facilitating the growth of online collaborative communication became an important strategy, along with ongoing support to overcome technical and policy issues as they arose.

The context and culture have been taken into account at each succeeding level: from international to national, then regional, local, and into individual schools. As this was developed, so were leadership and vision, and the continuing showcases and evaluations inform leadership and vision, the planning process, and the management of change. Lifelong learning, with a continuing focus on relevant pedagogy and educational objectives, was maintained within the vision, thus integrating the core competencies. Collaboration and networking were also modelled in the overall strategy.

Private Sector Initiatives

Intel Corporation has launched an international initiative to provide professional development resources to teacher educators in several countries. The programme is based on the Intel Teach to the Future programme begun January 2000 in the United States. The original programme provided training to in-service teachers on the integration of computer technology into teaching and learning. University faculty who worked with this in-service programme were so impressed by the quality and depth of the pedagogy and materials that they worked with Intel to develop a version of the programme that can be used at the university level with pre-service teachers.

Since then, the materials and curricula have been adapted to thirteen different languages including Spanish, Portuguese, English (British and US), Chinese, Hindi, Japanese, Korean, Urdu (Pakistan), German, Polish, Hebrew, and Russian. As a result, the programme is currently used in teacher preparation programmes in Argentina, Brazil, Canada, China, Costa Rica, Germany, India, Ireland, Italy, Mexico, Taiwan, United Kingdom, and the United States. There are plans to use Intel Teach to the Future in eleven additional countries within the next two years.

The ultimate goal of the Intel Teach to the Future programme is to engage elementary and secondary students in culturally and pedagogically appropriate learning experiences that are enhanced by using computers. "The core focus of this curriculum is to ensure that technology is used successfully to improve student learning." Teachers are guided to develop face-to-face, student-centred activities that model effective use of technology for teaching and learning. Faculty members who participate in this programme are recognised as curriculum experts. This programme helps them thoughtfully integrate their pedagogical expertise with computer technology.

The Intel Teach to the Future pre-service curricula are designed so that teacher educators and pre-service teachers can use it in a variety of learning Settings. Materials include paper and digital (CD-ROM) resources as well as Web support. Participants learn to use and integrate all three types of resources in their teaching and learning.

Topics covered include:

- — Developing and teaching technology-enhanced curricula
- — Locating and evaluating web resources
- — Copyright and citing of sources
- — Designing and creating multimedia presentations, desktop-published products, and web sites
- — Designing and creating teacher support materials
- — Developing plans for project implementation
- — Project development and assessment

Pre-service teachers learn to develop project plans, materials, and examples of student-created materials and presentations. For many teachers this involves a shift in approach from lecturer and expert to facilitator and learner. Examples created by participants are included with programme materials to assist other pre-service teachers as they develop their own plans and resources. Participants are encouraged to adapt these examples so that they reflect their knowledge of their own cultures. As local teachers develop new examples, they are added to the resource packet for their specific country. This adds relevance and role modelling, and encourages collaboration among pre-service teachers, their colleagues, and university faculty.

As they progress through the programme, pre-service teachers build on their existing technology skills, developing them as they develop their curricula. The central focus of this curricular approach is project planning. Working with a professor, who serves as facilitator, pre-service teachers develop project plans for elementary and secondary students that emphasise active learning and collaboration. Teachers are encouraged to develop learning activities that take advantage of the unique aspects of computer-based learning, such as creating interactive multimedia presentations and publications.

Using this approach, pre-service teachers are developing their own technology skills in an embedded and relevant way. For example, a pre-service teacher completing the programme will have achieved 85% of the skills required for the European Computer Driving License, but will have learned these skills as they relate to teaching and learning in the elementary and secondary classroom. They draw on their knowledge of their culture, language and curriculum to make sure that these activities are culturally appropriate and fit the overall goals of their education system.

One of the key elements of this programme is the view of faculty as curriculum experts. Participants begin by learning how to use the computer applications they will integrate into their programme plans. Then they identify a subject or concept they plan to teach and develop a project plan that integrates the use of computer technology. By starting with a topic they are familiar with, participants are better able to focus on identifying and developing resources and activities that serve as models of engaging learning activities for children. This familiarity leads to greater success and understanding of both technology and programme planning. As they develop their project plans, participants also develop the curriculum materials they will need to teach their lessons, resources that their students will use, and model examples of the projects their students will be creating. This provides faculty and pre-service teachers authentic experiences using technology and helps them better understand the processes and challenges their students will encounter when implementing their projects.

Throughout this experience, participants share their ideas and plans, discuss how they will assess student learning, and develop alternate activities so that their lessons can be used with a variety of students and settings. This reflective approach to teaching and learning further assures that pre-service teachers enter the classroom with the knowledge and skills needed to successfully integrate technology into culturally appropriate learning activities. The modular approach of this curriculum allows teacher education faculty to adapt it to their specific university programme. The full curriculum could be embedded in a single course, spread out over several courses, integrated into internship experiences, or some combination of all these.

To provide the greatest benefit, faculty who use this curriculum should be teacher education faculty who model the effective use of technology for teaching and learning as they teach the pedagogy of subjects. This helps pre-service teachers make the cognitive connections they need to further understand the teaching and learning process, and gives them the knowledge and skills they need to be effective educational leaders in their classrooms and schools.

SUPPORT TO ICTS IN TEACHER DEVELOPMENT

When a university, teacher education unit, state, region or country adopts or adapts a set of standards for determining how technology will be infused throughout their programmes, it is critical that faculty in the teacher education programmes be included in the planning effort. The faculty will plan for ICTs in teacher development considering their own conditions, culture, and context.

During this collaborative planning phase, the teacher education unit and other university units providing courses for pre-service teachers should develop plans that not only address the four key components within the framework, but also the elements that support long-term implementation of the key components-leadership and vision, context and culture, planning and management of change, and lifelong learning. These elements are necessary for a supportive environment and a successful, self-sustaining implementation of technology infusion within the teacher education programme.

Experience has shown that a number of essential conditions must be met to successfully integrate ICTs into teacher education programmes. As educational entities have implemented ICTs in teacher education, researchers and evaluators have identified barriers that prevent or restrict successful technology infusion. Teacher educators express frustration by stating, "I am having problems implementing our plan for infusion of ICTs because..." Such statements are often completed by one or more conditions quite common among teacher education institutions around the world.

When planning for implementation of ICTs in teacher education, the planning team should consider each essential condition and note whether, and to what extent, it is present. The context, culture, and extent of collaboration among stakeholders will affect how adequately the conditions are met and determine what types of strategies might solicit support if the essential conditions are not currently present.

Shared Vision

Defined as the presence of proactive leadership and administrative support, shared vision means that the commitment to technology is systemic. From the administration to the grounds personnel, there is an understanding of, commitment to, and sense of advocacy for the implementation of technology. When the implementation of a technology initiative is problematic, a major reason often cited is a breakdown in the common understanding of the institution's goals among those who hold the decision-making power. These situations can occur over something as simple as unlocking the door to a lab, or as complex as modifying existing operational budgets to provide allocations for technology funding. Facilitating the integration of technology may require a change in policy or rules, and the decision-makers have to be willing to look at the situation, forge compromises when necessary, and ensure communication among all parties. The collaborative environment necessary for creating a shared vision is also needed to sustain that vision.

Access

The fact that educators need access to current technologies, software, and telecommunications networks seems simple. However, this access must be consistent across all the environments that are part of the preparation of teachers. Most teacher education programmes involve several entities, including at least a college or university and one or more schools in the P-12 range. The access to funding and other resources may vary greatly among these partners, yet ideally, access should be adequate and consistent throughout the educational experience of students in the process of becoming teachers. Creative partnerships are often required to make this happen.

Skilled Educators

The educators who work with teacher candidates must be skilled in the use of technology for learning. They must be able to apply technology in the presentation and administration of their coursework and facilitate the appropriate use of technology by their teacher candidates. From the first course taken by a freshman, through collaborative work at the school site, pre-service teachers should participate with and observe their mentors using technology effectively. The teacher educator should model and teach techniques for managing technology in the classroom and for communicating outside the classroom through electronic means.

Professional Development

Even in contexts in which professional development is extensive, it is important to provide consistent access to professional development as the technology constantly changes. Ongoing opportunities for professional development should be available to university and P-12 faculty and administrators who participate in the preparation of teachers. The venues and delivery mechanisms should take into consideration issues of time, location, distance, credit options, and so on. Professional development is not a one-time event it should be focused on the needs of the faculty member, teacher, or administrator and sustained through coaching and periodic updates.

Technical Assistance

Educators need technical assistance to use and maintain technology. The focus of the faculty member, teacher, and pre-service teacher should be on teaching and learning, not on maintaining and repairing the technology beyond basic troubleshooting procedures. When the technology does not function well, a learning opportunity is lost and faculty frustration grows. Timely technical assistance is imperative for faculty and candidates to feel confident that they can use technology in their teaching and learning. There are many ways technical assistance can be obtained, including asking community members or student assistants to maintain a help desk. It is a critical factor for success in implementing ICTs.

Content Standards and Curriculum Resources

Educators must be knowledgeable in the content, standards, and teaching methodologies of their disciplines. Teacher candidates must learn to use technology in powerful, meaningful ways in the context of teaching content. Technology brings relevant resources from the real world to subject area content, provides tools for analysing and synthesising data, and conveys content through a variety of media and formats. Pre-service teachers should learn to use technology in ways that meet the content standards and the technology standards for students and teachers.

Student-Centred Teaching

Teaching in all settings should encompass student-centred approaches to learning. Technology should not be used only as a tool for demonstration, as an electronic overhead projector or blackboard; rather the use of technology by students should be an integral part of instruction. In student-centred approaches to learning, students become the source for problems investigated. Students and teacher candidates must have opportunities to identify problems, collect and analyse data, draw conclusions, and convey results using electronic tools to accomplish these tasks. Faculty should model the use of

ICTs to demonstrate their usefulness and appropriateness for collaboration, acquisition of resources, analysis and synthesis, presentation, and publication.

Assessment

In addition to assessing teaching and student outcomes, institutions should continuously assess the effectiveness of technology for learning throughout the entire teacher preparation environment. The data obtained from this continuous assessment will:

- — inform the learning strategies used,
- — ensure that the vision for technology-use maintains the appropriate direction,
- — pinpoint potential problems, and
- — provide data for altering policies and instructional strategies or for acquiring resources.

Changes made over time due to technology innovation will exemplify informed decision-making.

Community Support

The visioning process includes the community and school partners who provide expertise, support, and resources for technology implementation. The community must see that technology is a valuable tool for prospective teachers and their students, and must be willing to support it in the political process from the boardroom to the state house.

Support Policies

Policies can either support or hinder the implementation of technology. As decision-makers develop new policies, they must consider how the policies affect acquisition of and access to technology. Some major barriers to the use of technology relate to faculty expectations about incentives and reward structures.

Policies related to technical assistance should also support the use of technology rather than obstruct it. For example, although firewalls are essential in the university environment, there are ways to provide dial-up and remote access while maintaining the security of campus servers. Likewise, at the school level, there are ways to control students' Internet access to unwanted images and information while maintaining an environment of exploration and inquiry.

Teachers and teacher educators cannot be expected to implement what they have learned about effective use of ICTs without the presence of essential conditions in their work environment. The following environments correspond to stages of development commonly experienced during university preparation:

- *General Preparation*—General university courses providing instruction in the foundational courses for all students and the specific coursework in the student's major field of study.
- *Professional Preparation*—Formal coursework in professional education.
- *Student Teaching/Internship*—Supervised, extended field experience in the P-12 classroom.
- *First-Year Teaching*—The initial year of P-12 classroom teaching.

Recognition of the essential conditions necessary in all the environments that contribute to the preparation of teachers underscores the shared responsibility for preparing new teachers. The university, teacher education unit, and P-12 education must advocate resources that fulfil the essential conditions for each crucial stage of teacher development.

In planning the integration of ICTs into teacher education, it is important for teacher education institutions to understand the knowledge and skills necessary for teachers to effectively use ICTs in their instruction. They must also understand the institution's level of readiness to integrate technology into the teacher education curriculum. To accomplish these goals requires that the teacher education institution understand the benchmarks, standards, and guidelines for ICTs in teacher education. It is also important that they have access to tools that help them assess their level of readiness and progress in infusing ICTs into the teacher education programmes.

7

TRAINING OF WOMEN TEACHERS

Worldwide, the commitment to Education For All (EFA) is stronger than ever before. The Dakar Framework for Action plots a cour se towards EFA by 2015, with a key interim commitment to eliminate gender disparities in primary and secondary education by 2005. These commitments have been reinforced in the Millennium Development Goals (MDGs), and the International Development Targets (IDTs). The 1990 World Conference on Education for All, held in Jomtien, Thailand, proved to be a turning point for learners. Since that first EFA Forum, reform efforts in Universal Primary Education (UPE) have targeted girls and women above all other constituencies.

The International community's commitment to girls' education has become progressively more visible, vocal and focused on full and equal access to quality education for girls and boys. Some improvement in girls' enrolment followed the Jomtien Conference, but the decade leading up to the Millennium also brought difficult lessons that demonstrated a major gap worldwide between rhetoric and action. Deep and entrenched obstacles to girls' education went beyond inadequate resources, number of schools and female teachers.

A major shift in thinking, a major expansion of effort, and an all-encompassing movement to achieve relevant, quality education were required. Teachers needed not only gender-sensitive curricula and textbooks but also education in gender sensitivity. Teachers needed to devote broader, more overt attention to gender and to the underlying issues of poverty and discrimination. It was acknowledged that the presence of empowered teachers committed to gender equity in the classroom can be critical to the development of girls into empowered women. Gender-sensitive, empowered women teachers can serve as positive role models for girls and pass on new values to all their students.

CHANGING ROLE OF TEACHERS

To be involved in the dialogue about education systems around the world today is to understand and articulate the key role played by teachers. Through teachers can flow the ideology, values, and culture of a nation, state, and its people. Misinformation and constricted learning behaviours that students internalise can also be filtered through teachers' lack of knowledge, misjudgements, or biases. Calls for educational reform must therefore emphasise the education and empowerment of teachers that includes the real opportunity for them to share perspectives, power and decision-making.

One critical area in which all teachers must be educated is gender equity. Among international agencies and donors, EFA reform efforts have heavily targeted girls and women calling for the elimination of gender gaps in access, learning and retention. Numerous programmes have also been initiated that either focus entirely on females or make a special effort to ensure their inclusion. Education for girls, however, in strongly patriarchal countries will not result in empowered women who will participate in critical decision-making—unless their teachers are empowered supporters of gender equity. This is especially true of women teachers who must serve as positive role models.

Although they are the front-line participants and critical to successful quality schooling, teachers often form a silent majority; they are excluded not only from policy-making, governance and management, but also from day-to-day instructional strategies and decision making. Teachers as a whole, especially in less developed countries, have held minimal power in educational systems that are organised in hierarchical ways. Women teachers in particular are even less able to participate in decision-making and have even less voice in creating the institutional structures and policies that affect their lives—in and out of school—and the success of their students.

Education researchers point out that the structural and institutional aspects of schools, rather than teachers, perpetuate the barriers to empowerment and equity. Structural obstacles encourage the reproduction of current power relations rather than stimulate changes. Even in many educational reform efforts, for example, teachers are often the forgotten or taken-for-granted vehicles used to implement but not to create or initiate reforms. Pre-service and in-service training are often not planned or integrated into reform efforts; in many developing countries, teachers have no formal pre-service education at all.

Yet, in spite of these arguments, it is also true that in many countries teachers are becoming increasingly accepted as essential partners in a dynamic education system. But if efforts to increase student access, learning and retention in primary education are to succeed, relevant and empowering teacher education is crucial. Teachers must become active, fulfilled and empowered professionals themselves. If an educational system is to engender normative change, the entire system mus t be restructured to allow all actors to participate more democratically.

WOMEN'S TEACHER TRAINING AND GIRLS' EDUCATION

In India, the education system remains at a critical juncture. The world's second most populous country, with current estimates of over one billion people, India has a literacy rate of approximately 51 per cent. The history of India's educational system is complex, marked by deep debate and many contradictions between policy and practices and between laws and their enforcement. Elements of continuity and tradition have battled those of change and innovation. The power of cultural and historic barriers to change, including nearly two centuries of colonialism and many more centuries of a rigid caste system, have maintained a stubborn barrier to meaningful social transformation.

However, well before the past decade and even the past century, a populist movement continued to challenge very powerful traditional educational values and practices. A brief look at the diverse historical trends and currents can help to illuminate both the deep cultural roots of tradition and the strong reform elements that are critical to the current situation. This history reveals that progress is slow and uneven, and that the future is embedded in the past. Necessary changes must be perceived within the larger historical perspective.

Viewed through a gender lens, India's history of educational reform reveals more than a century of policies that seemed to anticipate and support the needed links between women's teacher education and education for girls. As early as 1882, the Indian Education Commission supported teacher-training institutes for women. In 1913, the Government Of India (GOI) passed a resolution that both established teaching universities and emphasised the education of girls.

Primary school teachers were required to pass a vernacular middle examination, receive one year of training and take refresher courses. They would receive a salary of not less than 12 rupees, (~35 cents) and teach classes with no more than 30 to 40 students. During the struggle for independence in 1947, and in the years following, a growing number of women activists struggled with the ideas of gender and social change, internally, with each other and with society. These women demanded a revision of the norms perpetuating inequities that would include the right to vote and equal rights to education.

In 1944, the women's literacy rate had grown only to 3.4 per cent from 0.9 per cent in 1901. Their demands went far beyond the goals of national leaders and male reformers who promoted a limited view of female education that left the basic patriarchal social structure unchanged. Male leaders aimed to "use education to make women more capable of fulfilling their traditional roles as wives and mothers and not to make them more efficient and active units in the process of socio-economic or political development". Gandhi himself advocated culturally suitable education for women: "There is need for similar distinction between the education of males and females as has been made between them by Mother Nature herself".

POLICY REFORMS

After independence, official GOI policies reflected the development of democratic ideology and institutions. The 1950 Constitution of independent India promised "universal, free, and compulsory education to all children up to the age of fourteen". Within this educational commitment, women were specifically named among "weaker others" to be given special protection and the opportunity to advance. To further these goals, the GOI established committees to reform the system including the Women's Education Committee, which addressed the training and employment of women teachers. Almost twenty years later, in 1968, India's first National Policy on Education (NPE) recommended that "the education of girls should require emphasis, not only on grounds of social justice, but also because it accelerates social transformation." This document also proposed raising the status and increasing the benefits and training of teachers.

The 1985 "Challenge of Education," a Ministry of Education policy perspective review, cited many shortcomings of the education system and criticised the government's failure to carry out reform. It drew attention to the continuing authoritarian, centralised and monolithic management approach that impeded decentralisation and local participation. The system, it said, also created an environment of anonymity and widespread apathy of teachers and the community in regard to primary school.

The role of teachers reflected the many, often opposing, currents of tradition, caste, colonialism and reform. On the one hand, teachers held the status of *guru* deriving from the *Brahman* ideal of moral authority and sacred knowledge, subduing the curiosity and questioning of students. Yet teachers received poor quality teacher training, low pay and had little decision-making power in regard to substantive or administrative issues. The Challenge of Education, also declared that: "...something will have to be done to change the orientation, work-ethic, knowledge and skills of the teachers, who will have to function much more creatively in a learning rather than a teaching environment, in which they will have to struggle continuously with new ideas as well as new technologies." The document also paid close attention to the quality of education, with a special focus on implementing child-centred and activity-based learning. Looking to education as an agent of basic change, the policy strengthened India's focus on girls' education and its link to women's empowerment. The education system would play an interventionist role in promoting women's studies and empowering women to become actively involved as decision makers and administrators.

The elimination of women's illiteracy and the removal of obstacles inhibiting their access to, and retention in, elementary education will receive overriding priority, through provision of special support services, setting of time targets, and effective monitoring. In 1992, further policy change continued to promote the end of gender discrimination and the empowerment of women to full participation. The NPE and Programme of Action (POA) viewed education as an instrument of social transformation that would eliminate curriculum biases and enable professionals such as teachers, decision makers, administrators and planners to play a positive interventionist role for gender equality. To achieve this would require a large-scale overhaul of policies and practices. Such measures included: training all teachers and instructors as agents of women's empowerment; developing gender and poverty sensitisation programmes for teacher educators and administrators; developing gender-sensitive curriculum; removal of sex bias from textbooks. They also included giving preference to female teacher recruitment to motivate parents to send girls to school. The NPE set explicit goals for women teachers' recruitment at a minimum of 50 per cent and urged that training facilities ensure an adequate, though unspecified, number of qualified women teachers in subjects that included mathematics and science.

Yet a stark contradiction has remained between policy commitments to women's equality and actual reform. Little real change has occurred despite the clear articulation by Indian educational policy and planning of what is necessary to create democratically structured programmes that will facilitate gender sensitivity and equity. Changing the ideology of a country steeped in cultural, social and economic inequities requires constant struggle. Over the years, the absence of political initiative and funding accompanied by changes in political control has hindered steady progress toward these goals. Women's national literacy rates remain at 42 per cent compared to the rate of 69 per cent for men.

Acknowledging these discouraging statistics, the Indian POA (1992) argues that the will to implement institutional mechanisms to ensure the reflection of gender sensitivity in educational programmes is still strongly needed. The limited scope of women's roles must be replaced with a 21st century ideology that makes them full participants in socio-economic and political development. Programmes that attempt to incorporate gender equitable policies, including those for teachers, have been increasing. Because they play a pivotal role in transmitting equality to their students, women teachers must be high on the list of women who participate in more gender equitable programmes.

TEACHER EMPOWERMENT PROGRAMME (TEP)

The Teacher Empowerment Programme emerged as one important programme that focused increasingly on gender equity for teachers. This in-service programme began in the Dhar district of Madhya Pradesh in 1992 as a grassroots effort designed to meet the immediate needs of teachers for new content and skills that would increase their influence on the process of education. Focused on interactive participation and decision-making of teachers, the TEP aimed to place power in their hands and facilitate its responsible use. Innovative and imaginative, the TEP did not reject official education policy; its general objectives and processes are consistent with the guidelines of the National Policy on Education (NPE) and its Programme of Action (POA).

The TEP began as a UNICEF initiative yet was enabled through a long standing relationship with the Government of India, familiarity with government policies and practices, and a deep understanding of the needs and conditions of teachers. Through combined goals and efforts, the partnership of UNICEF, the GOI, and the teachers' union capitalised on an increasingly conducive environment and was able to put stated policy goals into practice. For teachers, this meant improved status, teaching skills and materials, greater participation and decision-making in governance and programme development and more joyful training in pedagogy. The empowerment of teachers would also have a direct and positive bearing on achieving the goals for students that included increased attendance, retention through class five—especially for girls—and higher levels of achievement. According to Jude Henriques, the UNICEF education officer at the forefront of the TEP's initial development, most education reforms begin with the curriculum, textbooks, and testing procedures. For him, reform begins with the teacher.

The TEP ties educational developmental theory to practice as teachers learn a child-responsive approach that is joyful and experiential. They learn that teachers must be nurturing and caring and offer concrete contexts so children can learn through play and various hands-on activities. They learn to provide opportunities for children to express themselves verbally and artistically through singing, dancing, and drama and to allow ample time to tell and listen to stories that make sense of their environment and their lives.

Unlike most previous in-service trainings, the TEP addresses the lack of joy in teaching, the overburdened curriculum and the unmotivated teachers—all criticisms in various GOI and other education reports. The unshakeable foundation of the Joyful Learning approach is that teachers participate and collaborate through an interactive, hands-on approach. The choice of districts in which to implement the TEP was linked to indicators showing the poorest literacy rates. UP is India's most populous state and one of the five lowest literacy states where the rate stands at about only 41 per cent—55 per cent for males and only 25 per cent for females.

When the TEP expanded to the State of UP, teachers themselves chose the name Ruchipurna Shikshan or Joyful Learning (JL) for their training, reflecting both their ownership of the programme and a new attitude it motivated. Just one month before the training began in UP, on the day annually celebrated as Teachers' Day, over 12,000 teachers pledged and committed themselves to work toward UPE, to avoid absenteeism and drunkenness, and to become better teachers. Since that day, many teachers have pledged or re-pledged their commitment as part of the Joyful Learning Programme.

Among the ways in which Henriques promoted the effectiveness of the TEP was to make sure that teachers could participate at low cost and to emphasise activities that were concrete and relevant to the local environment. Teachers made their own teaching aids such as the cloth pocket board sewn to create rows and pockets. They used colour-coded cards for activities such as matching, categorising, and sequencing, or word cards that enabled language arts skills such as vocabulary, syntax, or story telling. These activities have remained a part of the training throughout the history of the programme, and flourish today. Low-cost, low-tech and inclusive processes represent activities that teachers can initiate with the children themselves. The portable, pocket board teaching aid has proven particularly effective in environments where there is no classroom.

Yet just as important as providing teachers with new skills and content, the training in UP went beyond teachers and administrators. It included space for dialogue among teachers, trainers and government officials for reflection, sharing and discussion of concerns. In one training session, for example, teachers expressed concern about outdated syllabi and curricula in the pre-service Basic Teacher Training (BTT) programme. They expressed the need for better communication among department officials, monitors, and the DIET (District Institute of Education and Training) instructors to increase their understanding and ownership of the TEP. The intangible aspects and principles upon which the programme was based are evident during these dialogues—respect, trust, commitment, and equity.

Teachers are all creative, talented people and respond remarkably when they are respected and included in the decision-making integral to their work in the classroom. They gain a sense of ownership over their work and their classrooms, when they are involved in development of the curriculum, designing of the syllabus, making and selecting of teaching materials and in designing training programmes leading to their own intellectual and professional development.

Placing teachers in a central role, encouraging hands-on interactive activities and the making of teaching aids have garnered strong and wide teacher support in the districts in which the programme has operated. Although implementation is challenging, partners have learned to work together and make the best use of each others' diverse expertise, resources and knowledge. Furthermore, the TEP has begun to converge with other government-sponsored teacher training programmes to spread more widely the joyful learning that ultimately will benefit both the teachers and the students.

TEP AND WOMEN TEACHERS

Over the past three decades as feminist research has taken on an abstract and theoretical quality, its origins are often forgotten—origins based in the lifeblood and 'lived realities' of women's experience. As women's lives keep changing, this earthbound educational reform programme in India is a reminder that change is slow and uneven and that to become empowered women themselves must keep reliving, reviewing and revising their experience. The following precepts bring together feminist principles with the TEP experience.

Worldwide, and for several decades, the critical role of female teachers in reducing the gender gap in primary and secondary education has been well established. Numerous studies indicate that girls in developing countries "learn better and stay in school longer when their teachers are women". The general assumption had been that the presence of female teachers would provide an automatic incentive for girls to enrol in school; they would create a safe atmosphere that would encourage families to send their daughters to school, and would provide positive role models. Simply because they were women, female teachers would be gender sensitive in their attitudes and behaviours, fight for more gender sensitive curriculum and provide a safe environment free from sexual harassment. An increase in the numbers of women teachers would accelerate, if not ensure, sustainable gender equality in education.

The 1950 Indian Constitution guaranteed free, universal, compulsory education for all children to the age of 14 with female education as a key element of planned development. Yet today, girls in India still conspicuously trail their male counterparts. India has the largest number of out of school girls in the world—over 19.5 million. Current figures suggest that there are over 11 million fewer girls than boys enrolled at the primary level. Literacy rates are 69 per cent for men and only 42 per cent for women.

Many approaches have been put in place to reduce this gap-awareness campaigns, child-care centres, more schools closer to home, direct incentives. Experience has proven repeatedly that there is strength in numbers. When a country's teacher education programmes graduate enough female teachers, the likelihood of expanding female education improves. In fact, the Education for Women's Equality chapter of India's 1992 POA notes the direct relationship between dropout rates of girls and the small proportion of women teachers.

In the state of UP, which has one of the lowest literacy rates in India, female teachers number only 21 and 23 per cent in rural primary and middle level schools. In urban areas, these percentages are 56 and 57 per cent. Achieving a critical mass can give groups of excluded members of society mutual support and the motivation to speak out, assert themselves and express in the public sphere what has been for protection only private attitudes and behaviours. Continued exposure of men to large numbers of women on an equal footing will help them to stop seeing women as subordinate and to accept change.

Experience has also shown that hiring more women teachers will not by itself promote gender equity and social change. As long as societal gender discrimination persists, access alone will neither keep girls in school nor produce empowered women capable of significant decisionmaking. Women themselves internalise and replicate the lessons of culture. They carry with them and pass on to girls under their tutelage the societal behaviours and attitudes imposed on them from early childhood. They do this, often unintentionally or unknowingly, through their own culturally determined behaviours and attitudes.

As role models, women teachers may communicate to girls the dictates to be obedient or submissive, not to stand up for themselves or take risks. In the classroom, research has shown repeatedly that women teachers may also perpetuate these behaviours and pass on traditional messages by calling on boys first and allowing, even encouraging, interruption, argumentativeness and other traditionally male behaviours while discouraging girls from the same behaviours. Educators themselves need to be empowered supporters of gender equity and of women teachers who will serve as positive role models. These possibilities imply social transformation and, thus, threaten the existing power structure.

If women are to achieve equality in Indian society, women teachers must be in the forefront of those who encourage social transformation for girls. They must themselves be, and help young females to be, critically aware of their society's norms that include an understanding of patriarchy and how and why females have been traditionally subordinated in society. They must help female students to challenge accepted gender roles. "Activism should not ignore the interplay between the empowering and the oppressive in the form and content of our work".

Empowerment has become an important concept in the work of many agencies. It is consistent with the shift in approach from Women in Development (WID)—a gender neutral demand for women's equal integration into the development process—to Gender in Development (GID-also often called Gender and Development, GAD) which demands a change in structural relations to create greater power and autonomy. When women both participate and express their views, and have the power to make decisions that affect their public and personal lives, they are empowered.

Teacher empowerment programmes that incorporate GID theory promote these goals. It is argued that empowered women teachers lead to greater retention and learning achievement for girls. More critically conscious, educated women can contribute to a more just and equitable social order that includes transformation as a goal of educational reform.

Feminist scholarship has shown repeatedly how the patriarchal construction of knowledge devalues both the intellect and emotions of females. Educational systems are microcosms of societal values and formal education. Their function is to instill appropriate behaviour and cultural norms, which often includes unspoken but clear gender-specific messages. Schools then, at all levels, are too often vehicles for reproducing stereotyped or limited views of girls and boys, women and men.

Examining the issues through women's personal experience, or what is called 'lived realities', helps to better expose and understand the depth of gender messages and how women's private lives and roles are both mirrored in and hidden from the public sphere. Documenting women's realities and making their lives visible helps to expose and correct the patriarchal bias of social science. Conceptualising women's private behaviour as an expression of cultural and societal dictates has enabled feminist researchers to bring a persuasive new perspective to the theory of political and social power relations. It also allows women, who understand their own experiences in a new way, to contribute to the creation of a new social order that benefits women, girls and all society. For both men and women, discussion and exploration of experiential forms of expression often result in a better grasp of the strong links between private and public realms.

Underlying the implementation of the TEP is the philosophy that teachers must be trusted, respected, listened to, and encouraged to nurture their creative abilities. Committed to the empowerment of all teachers, trainers in the earliest sessions in Madhya Pradesh did not include explicit discussion of gender, caste or class issues. No content explicitly targeted excluded populations, structural inequalities and obstacles or patriarchy. The emphasis was on the immediate participation of all teachers through activities that encourage open and equal male and female interaction and break down inhibitions that would obviate the need for specific attention to gender issues.

This mainstreaming, or gender blind, strategy prevalent at the start of the movement for gender equality, acknowledged the need for equal female participation but emphasised that programmes should respond to the needs and concerns of women within the framework of broader human and social development objectives. However, such an approach has also exposed the difficulties of translating mainstreaming goals into visible results and actions and has proven extremely limited in producing significant and speedy improvement in the status of women. This is true in the most socially progressive societies, but especially in country programmes where the national environment is not conducive to promoting social equity and empowerment of women.

Looking at the TEP through a gender lens, what arises as central to the discussion are the relative benefits and drawbacks to mainstreaming gender concerns through gender-neutral practices of equality or to promoting gender-specific analysis and activities. What some call gender neutral or gender-blind approaches to the training do not consciously promote or directly raise awareness of the larger societal, structural inequalities that must be altered.

8

TEACHER EDUCATOR TRAINING

Education and training of teacher educators is a pre-requisite for effective changes in the training and orientation of teachers. India has a large system of teacher education. There are more than 2000 elementary teacher education institutions, Colleges of Education and University Departments of Education. Nearly 30,000 teacher educators are engaged in the preparation of school teachers. In addition, there are teacher educators working in pre-primary training schools as well as institutions concerned with the preparation of teachers for the education of children with special needs and alternative education.

The overall quality in education mainly depends on the quality of teachers and a sound programme of professional preparation of teachers is essential for imparting quality education. However, teacher educators' own education leaves much to be desired. Teaching is an art which can be inculcated through a series of well designed activities in respect of education and training of teachers and is equally valid for professional preparation of teacher educators. The teacher educators would not only be training pre-service and in-service trainees but would also be associating themselves with several other activities.

New strategies and techniques of material development, the changing approach to evaluation, intensive interactions with the community, creating an activity-based environment in the training institutions, acquiring skills for resource mobilisation and several other such competencies at mastery level would be essential for professionals to function as teacher educators. Changes in the school curricula would be faster in the near future. Corresponding changes in training programmes and strategies shall have to be perceived and given a shape by the teacher educators.

In the context of universalisation of elementary education, teacher educators will be expected to display a deeper understanding of the issues pertaining to access, participation and attainment in their specific regions or areas. They need adequate professional competence to conduct such surveys and studies would reveal the region specific and area specific issues and problems which would help the functionaries of the education department and the community. They will prepare the trainees in responding to these issues during the training period and also in schools subsequently.

The professional quality of teacher educator will determine the quality of the training of teachers, both pre-service as well as in-service. The professional level at which teachers are prepared would, in turn, determine the quality of school education. Again, teacher educators have to be fully familiar with the school realities, social environment and community expectations to realistically perform the challenging tasks before them. On the professional side, teacher educators need to be actively associated with policy formulations, implementation strategies and monitoring of programmes.

PROGRAMME FOR TEACHER EDUCATORS

In India, the only programme which is often treated as preparing teacher educators is that of M.Ed. Scrutiny of the curriculum of most of the M.Ed. programmes would reveal that these have not been specifically designed to prepare teacher educators. There are some M.Ed. programmes where provisions do not exist for writing a dissertation. The products of these programmes would certainly not be in a position to conduct research, initiate innovation on their own and induct teacher trainees in these areas which are essential functions of teacher educators. Prior to the establishment of the NCTE as a statutory body, NCERT acted as its secretariat and organised several professional development programmes for teacher educators in areas like micro-teaching and simulation, student teaching and evaluation, preparing research proposals, improvement of teacher education curricula and so on.

The University Grants Commission (UGC) has been organising national and regional level workshops for improvement of the teacher education programmes. Through various schemes it offers financial support for seminars, workshops and research projects for teacher educators for such themes as higher education, educational technology, non-formal education, population education, environmental education, research methodology, etc.

The National Institute of Educational Planning and Administration (NIEPA) organises programmes for Principals of Colleges of Education, Heads of University Departments of Education and other administrators concerned with teacher education. The SCERTs and State Boards of Teacher Education organise continuing education programmes for teacher educators on teaching methodologies for new subject areas and on innovations in education.

Some University Departments of Education organise seminars, workshops, and orientation programmes for teacher educators on teaching, development of instructional skills, interaction analysis, teaching behaviour, educational technology, guidance and counselling and research methodology. Certain Colleges of Education and University Departments of Education have been upgraded as Colleges of Teacher Education (CTEs) and Institutions of Advanced Study in Education (IASEs) for taking up innovations in teacher education.

NCTE after its establishment in 1995 as a statutory body, has initiated several programmes aimed at enhancing professional competence of teacher educators. These include seminars and workshops in the area of human rights and national values, indigenous thoughts in education, indigenous approach to teacher preparation, institutional networking and capacity enhancement and production of good quality enrichment materials for teacher educators. These institutions have considerable experiences in organising training and development activities. Based upon the experience gained they will have to evolve programmes of sequential nature with in-built mechanism for assessment and impact evaluation.

In the absence of an appropriate policy of recruitment, specially at the pre-primary, primary and elementary stages of teacher preparation, the manpower in the institutions of teacher education does not necessarily possess the professionally required qualifications for the preliminary stages.

At the pre-primary stage one comes across teacher educators who have passed high school or higher secondary examination and possess a certificate in teacher training, not necessarily meant for the pre-primary stage; graduates or those with higher qualification with absolutely no training background or with the background not appropriate for that stage or level.

As regards the primary and elementary stages, the teacher educators, generally, possess graduate or higher qualification with teacher training mostly at the B.Ed. level. There are serious lacunae in the recruitment policies in as much as the professional qualifications prescribed are not stage-specific and mostly not suited to the education of teachers for the stage or level concerned. This situation calls for fresh thinking regarding recruitment policies for teacher educators and well-planned programmes of education for teacher educators.

RATIONALE OF TRAINING TEACHER EDUCATORS

Education and training of teacher educators has to focus its attention on the new role of teacher educators on the problems which reflect the emerging global trends in education and the overall needs and aspirations of the people in India. It has also to deal with specific problems confronting teacher education institutions and to make teacher education more responsible and responsive. It also has to encourage teacher educators' continuing professional growth.

In addition, there are certain practical problems as well. For instance , what would be the basic qualifications of teacher educators at various stages of teacher preparation? What would be the requirements in respect of the core education courses and for the organisation of procedures and practices in the institutions. Answers to several of such issues have to be sought in the very rationale of providing professional education.The rationale behind the education and professional training of teacher educators lies in providing qualitative instruction through well-designed programmes of professional education.

The following questions are relevant for designing a programme for education of teacher educators:

— What exactly should the education of teacher educators aim at?

— What are the significant issues and problems concerning the education of teacher educators?

— What are the possible models of both pre-service as well as inservice education of teacher educators?

— What patterns, contents and techniques are envisaged?

— What are the possible agencies and organisations which could be profitably employed in providing continuing abd recurrent inservice education to teacher educators?

The following objectives can be comprehensively identified for the programmes of preparation of teacher educators :

— to develop competencies and skills needed for preparation of teachers and teacher educators

— to enable them to organise competency-based and commitment oriented professional programmes

— to enable them to develop pedagogy relevant to the education of teacher educators

— to acquire an understanding of the needs and problems of teacher educators and teacher education institutions

— to develop skills related to management of teacher education institutions

— to develop competencies of curriculum development and preparation of learning and evaluation materials

— to enable teacher educators to acquire capabilities to organise in-service continuing education programmes

— to enable them to organise need-based and commitment oriented on the job training

— to develop competencies for evaluating educational programmes and teaching learning materials

— to develop the capacity of examination, analysis, interpretation, elaboration and communication of educational ideas

— to relate education and the national needs and develop critical awareness about Indian realities

— to enable them to understand the relationship between Indian ethos, modern technology and education

— to promote the global perspective of educational development with special reference to the developing countries.

— to enable them to undertake meaningful educational research.

— to develop the capacities to reinterpret Indian heritage, culture and values to meet the requirements of the present-day Indian society.

— to develop the capabilities for self-directed and life-long learning.

— to enable them to appreciate and adopt emerging communication technology and innovative practices in Indian context.

PRE-SERVICE TRAINING OF TEACHER EDUCATORS

The present system of pre-service education of teacher educators is characterised by lack of perspective in terms both of contents as well as qualifications. For instance, while it is well accepted that the B.Ed. qualification entitles a person to teach at secondary stage, it is doubtful if the M.Ed. programme adequately prepares a person to become teacher of secondary school teachers. The existing M.Ed. programme has little provision of training in and working out teaching and evaluation strategies suited to the needs of teacher trainees. And yet one finds M.Ed. degree holders entrusted with the responsibility of teacher preparation not only at secondary stage but also at the pre-primary, primary and elementary stages of teacher preparation.

Likewise, while the B.Ed. qualification legitimately entitles a person to teach at the secondary stage, it cannot, at the same time, be accepted as a good enough qualification for being a teacher educator at the primary stage. The existing B.Ed. programme is designed mainly to teach high school students and not for preparing primary school teacher educators. Thus, it is imperative that the professional qualification of teacher educators is made stage-specific suited to the needs of teacher trainees of different categories.

Education of teacher educators has necessarily to correspond to teacher preparation programmes. It is nonetheless necessary to consider alternatives and institute programmes like M.Ed. (Teacher Education) catering to the needs of stage-specific and category-specific preparation of teacher educators alongside general M.Ed. programmes. M.Ed. (Teacher Education) could be conducted for the following specific categories and areas:

— M.Ed. (Pre-primary)

— M.Ed. (Elementary)

— M.Ed. (Secondary & Sr. Secondary)

— M.Ed. (Special Education)

— M.Ed. (Distance Education)

— M.Ed. (Physical Education)

Existing M.Ed. courses in Indian Universities are by and large academic in nature and not adequately professional in content. In as much as the Master's level courses in Education need to be formulated for making it a professional course, some additional areas of study will have to be introduced with changed orientation.

The course structure in respect of the above alternative M.Ed programmes has to correspond to the course structure of teacher education at various stages and categories. For instance, the M.Ed (Elementary) programme may comprise the following courses.

- — Contemporary Indian Society
- — Philosophy of Education
- — Educational Sociology, Social and Cultural Anthropology
- — Child Psychology including the researches in life and medical sciences having bearing on elementary education and psychology of teaching and learning with reference to child
- — Curriculum Development, Transaction and Evaluation
- — Comparative Education with reference to developed and developing countries.
- — Pedagogical Analysis of School Subjects
- — Research Methodology
- — Dissertation
- — Field Work, Practical and Internship.

STRENGTHENING TEACHER TRAINING PROGRAMMES

Needless to say that the preparation of teacher educators would concern itself with the relevant theoretical courses as well as the consonant practicum. At the theoretical level, the choice of pedagogical inputs has to be guided by various contexts and their educational and professional concerns. In addition to theory courses, specialisation courses with reference to teacher education have to be included. The theoretical courses will have a bearing on the practice of teacher education. It will be necessary to develop competencies and skills in prospective teacher educators relating to their work situations. What goes on in teacher training institutions by way of educational programmes and activities has to be reflected in the education and training of teacher educators. It essentially implies that the preparation of teacher educators has to be made an integral part of the system of teacher education.

It will be pertinent to evolve a pedagogy relevant to the stage or category specific programmes. It will lay due emphasis on societal goals, values specially those enshrined in the Indian Constitution, higher order learning processes, curriculum development and theory and practice of educational research including action research. Competence to carry out research and innovations needs to be acquired by all. Training in curriculum development and preparation of learning materials is inalienable aspect of entire process of teacher education. Similarly, development of evaluation materials would result into more effective utilisation of evaluation in teacher education institutions.

The practical work has among other things necessarily to include internship programme by way of attachment to the stage-specific and category-specific teacher education institutions. This will give the prospective teacher educators an adequate knowledge of the total functioning of teacher education institution, the improvements needed and also provide insights into the problems and issues concerning maintenance of institutional plant, classroom management, organisational climate of the institution etc.

As for practice teaching, the main thrust has to be on a variety of techniques such as team teaching, micro-teaching, panel discussion, seminar, demonstration, etc. as integral part of classroom-teaching-learning-evaluation procedures. Practical work other than internship and practice teaching has to develop competencies and skills in organising activities concerning work education and working with community as per the practical work requirements in the teacher education institutions.

The present provision for continuing education of teacher educators is inadequate in respect of both quality and content. Planning in respect of in-service education of teacher educators needs to be evolved for different stages and levels. The major thrusts in respect of programmes for teacher educators among others, may be as follows:

— Designing short-term programmes for those who are already placed in these institutions.

— Specific short-term induction programmes for those who do not have the experience for the stage they are supposed to be working at.

— Identification of certain university departments of education and Institutions of Advanced Study in Education as institutions which may work mainly for teacher educators. They may focus on induction training, recurrent training, orientation programmes, research studies and surveys, curriculum development, preparation of training materials, evaluation strategies and techniques, use of educational technology, media and others.

— Establishment of institutions for preparation of teacher educators for special education at different stages. These may be open to primary and secondary trained graduates willing to become teacher educators. Such programmes need to be designed with particular focus on the practicum that would familiarise the trainees with school situations in totality.

— Networking of various institutions and organisations for designing and carrying out collaborative programmes by pooling and sharing of resources.

With the policy focus changing to quality and relevance of education, it is necessary that only those, who are professionally competent, committed and willing, are charged with the responsibility of preparing teachers for the nation. Teachers for various stages, levels and categories are prepared professionally by teacher educators. The quality and character of teachers therefore, would largely depend on the professional education of teacher educators. Towards this, it is necessary, therefore, that their education should be given a new orientation and improved qualitatively and adjusted properly with the demands of the new curriculum.

9

VALUE ORIENTATION IN TEACHER TRAINING

We are passing through a great transition. The old is becoming obsolete and the new is still in the process of emergence. The old ways of learning and teaching are found to be too rigid and too out-moded. A greater application of psychological principles is being increasingly demanded. It has been urged that the training of the young requires on the part of the teacher a deep psychological knowledge.

According to some thinkers, the present educational system is a huge factory of mis-education. According to them the spontaneity of the child is smothered at an early stage by our mechanical methods which are prevalent in our education system. They contend that the child is not a plastic material which can be moulded according to educators' design, but it is a closed bud having its own inherent capacity to flower and blossom, needing only the favourable climate conditions such as the right atmosphere, environment, inspiration and guidance.

Each child is a psychological entity, having its own specific individual needs of growth which have to be understood and developed by the same kind of knowledge and tact by which a good gardener tends varieties of plants and trees in his garden. Just as each plant needs to be individually looked after, even so, each child, it is contended, is required to be looked after individually. It has been further held that each individual is a great potential dynamo of energy, and if we do not deal with that potentially, only very little gets actualised, and the rest remains dormant and uncultivated. This means a tremendous waste both for the nation and the world. Not to tap the full potentialities of each individual is thus psychologically unsound and economically unproductive. It has, therefore, been urged that our educational system should either be set aside altogether through some kind of 'deschooling" or radically changed in such a way that each individual is provided with conditions and facilities under which he can grow towards his fullness on the lines that are psychologically appropriate to him.

There is another line of thinking according to which it is not enough to develop the potentialities of the individual but also to direct these potentialities towards their highest values. It has been argued that the psychological development of the individual is an extremely dangerous process, unless the development is guided by wisdom and skill and directed towards certain desirable and sublime ideals. There is a risk, it is argued, of succeeding in developing only highly egoistic and selfish individuals, if we insist only upon development and do not take a great care to insist on the discovery of the right values, aims, objectives and ideals. It has, therefore, been urged that education should be value-oriented and should provide those conditions and facilities under which each individual is enabled to discover the highest possible values and enbody them as effectively as possible in thought, feeling and action.

An unprecedented education experiment which is taking place in different parts of the world today has resulted in the formulation on new models of learning-teaching process. It has been argued that learning is a process of transmutation, transmutation of innate reflexes into organised and conscious perceptions, visions and actions, transmutation of innate drives into wise and skillful pursuit of means and ends, and transmutation of innate tendencies into a harmonious integrated personality. It has been contended that there are observable and discernible processes by which the process of learning or of transmutation can be accelerated.

We are often asked to consider the tremendous feat of learning that the child performs in the first few years of its life. It has been contended that the child learns so fast because all its occupations are occupations of learning. For the child, all play is learning, and all learning is a play. Again, it is contended, the child learns so fast because the child deals with its universe with its total being by the exercise of all its faculties and by a concrete urge of experience. It has been argued that our entire learning process should be so changed that we are able to create for the learner the same conditions which obtain in the child's encounter with its universe. Some educationists have, therefore, pleaded for a search of a school that has no walls, and for studies that have no boundaries.

The learner learns best under the conditions of freedom to choose, under teacher's wise guidance, what he wants to learn and what he should learn. The learner should have also the freedom of pursuing his studies at his own pace. This argument is further intensified when it is seen that an indispensable condition of the moral and spiritual development is secured only when the learner is given ample opportunities to exercise his free will. Learning by doing is being increasingly advocated. At the same time, it is being recognised that there are, for different categories of learners, different ways of learning.

Some students learn better through aesthetic experience, some others through manual work, while still others through intellectual or meditative contemplation. It has, therefore, been suggested that an ideal system of education should provide to each learner that method or such combination of methods which is suitable to his specific needs of learning.

Self-learning is being given in several experiments a pre-eminent place. Individualised programmed instruction, for example, follows an instructional model which aspires to produce an effective communication for securing precisely defined goals of learning, in a manner timed to meet the needs of the individual, mostly with the help of programmed teaching and learning material. An important variant of individualised learning is that of learning of consultation with the teacher, as and when needed. Lecture system, which caters to group learning, plays a minor role in experiments which emphasise self-learning. Even the syllabi and examination system are required to be radically changed in the context of a system based upon self-learning.

Project systems try to combine self-learning with group-learning. Projects may be directed towards an exploration or towards producing some practical action under certain actual situations. In a model that is known as Info-Bank, the learner is required to define what he is interested in and the kind of approach that he wants to undertake. The learner is given the freedom to govern his reading and practical activities and to judge the knowledge acquired and its significance. In some educational experiments, a combination of different information materials is made available to the learner and he is given the freedom to construct and control his own learning process and the environment suitable for the chosen learning process. In yet another instructional model, individual learners learn from one another by informing and consulting one another mutually from time to time.

At a higher level of consultation, there is experimental testing and feed-back. In some models, the learner takes over the roles of those responsible for action and decision in simulated environment. In some cases, problems to be solved are frequently more complex and make the acquisition of external information necessary, while in others the required information is supplied in advance. In the "Workshop Model", the learners work like colleagues, supported, if necessary, by organisers and advisers, on the solution of real problems with which they are confronted. In this model, the learning of the methods of work is as important as the production of results.

Educationists are perplexed by the phenomenon of un-precedented explosion of knowledge. Teachers and learners are required to deal with this explosion, and efforts are being made to discover accelerated methods of learning and teaching. The necessity of continuous or life-long education is also being underlined. At the same time, teachers and students are required to distinguish more clearly than ever before, those aspects of knowledge which are essential from those which are of peripheral importance. There is also today an unparalleled width and depth of enquiry, which necessitates a new kind of learning-teaching process that would be at once comprehensive and yet peculiarly specialised or varied so as to suit each individual.

Again, there is today a great quest all over the world towards the synthesis of knowledge and synthesis of culture. Ancient knowledge is being recovered in the context of the modern knowledge. The humanist and the technologist are finding themselves in greater and greater need of each other. It is being increasingly recognised that the learner should not only develop his rational faculties but should also pursue moral and aesthetic tendencies. In India, we go farther and underline the need of a synthesis of science and spirituality. Against this background, there is a quest to discover a point of convergence where different sciences and humanities can meet in a synthesis of knowledge. There is a search for an all-embracing project of work-experience that would generate a continuing process of life-long education. And there is a search for a programme of learning that would necessitate a spontaneous harmony of the needs of a personal development with the needs of collective development.

It is being asked if there is a tool of the acceleration of the summing up of the past and the unfolding of the future. And it is asked if there is a method and content of education that would necessitate an automatic synchronisation of studies, work-experience and flowering of faculties and values. It has become necessary, both for the learner and for the teacher, to discover or invent such methods by the employment of which the explosion of knowledge can be contained and personality can be developed which would harmonise, progressively, the wideness of the humanist and the skill of the technologist, the disciplined will-force of the moralist and the refined imagination of the artist, and the scrupulous knowledge of the scientist and the sublime vision, wisdom and ever-growing perfection of the profound and wide spiritual culture.

There are today powerful trends that necessitate a continual revision of the contents of education as also a continual refinement of the learning-teaching process. It is against this background that there is a serious thinking in our country to determine the new role that the teacher is called upon to play. The situation in India is in a sense more complex than in many other countries of the world. India is passing through a tremendous period of scientific and cultural efflorescence. This period was marked by a powerful phase of the national freedom struggle during which the Indian sub-continent passed through an unprecedented churning of mental, aesthetic, moral and spiritual ideas. In the course of this churning, profound experiments in the field of education took place, the lessons of which need still to be assimilated.

There grew in India during this period an irresistible sentiment to give to the children and the youths of our country a new kind of education, which is freed from the letters of the system given to us by the British and which would ensure development and promoting among students and teachers not only of the highest values of physical, emotional, mental, aesthetic, moral and spiritual culture, but also those values which are uniquely Indian, and which would at the same time promote a new kind of synthesis appropriate to our own composite culture. India has developed a kind of secularism which needs to be properly defined, understood and promoted. We have to build up young men and women who would have pride in the Indian heritage and our composite culture.

BASIC CONCEPTS

The word value as understood in the context of educational philosophy refers to those desirable ideals and goals which are intrinsic in themselves and which, when achieved or attempted to be achieved, evoke a deep sense of fulfilment to one or many or all parts of what we consider to be the highest elements of our nature. In a sense, it may be urged that the word value is basically undeniable, since it denotes a fundamental category and it is itself the highest genus of that category. At the same time, there is a common understanding among all of us as to what we mean when it is said that Truth, Beauty and Goodness are the supreme value of life. They are intrinsic in character and they are ends of themselves.

They are considered to be the most desirable ideals and they occur to us whenever we try to conceive of those states of our being or becoming in which we are likely to find some kind of ultimate fulfilment.

All true education is fundamentally a process of training whereby the individual is enabled to embody progressively, those values which we in our highest thought and aspiration come to regard as something most desirable. If we analyse our human nature, we find there are in us various energies which can be distinguishable under various categories, such as physical, emotional, mental, aesthetic, moral and spiritual. These energies are mostly latent in us and only a part of them are actually active. Even the active part of our energies needs to be developed and directed towards their highest point of fulfilment in their respective values. But the task of education is not limited merely to the development of our active energies but also to bring out our latent capacities and lead them to their rightful goals and ideals.

The teacher should therefore have a sound knowledge of the psychology of man and should know the secrets of the principles underlying the development of both our active and latent capacities. In our present system of education, we are too preoccupied with the mental development of the development, we give a preponderant importance to those qualities which are relevant to our present examination system. We are thus giving not so much of importance to the development of the powers of understanding as to the power of memory. We do not emphasis the development of imagination as much as we emphasis the power of knowing facts. We do not give importance to the pursuit of Trust as much as to the pursuit of piece-meal assemblage of topics and subjects which are prescribed in our syllabus. Recently, attempts have been made to ameliorate this situation and some place is being given to physical education and aesthetic education. But the situation is far from satisfactory, and when we come to the domain of moral and spiritual values, the situation is confusing and it seems, a deeper exploration is required before we give to ourselves some definite idea as to what they mean and what place they can be given in our system of education.

The situation in regard to moral and spiritual values is complicated by the fact that there are today several powerful trends of thought in the light of which morality has come to be regarded as something relative and spirituality is being dismissed as some undeniable category of irrationalism. It is sometimes held that scientific method is the only door to knowledge, while morality and spirituality can at best be a kind of emotional responses.

It is, therefore, sometimes argued that what needs to be advanced in our educational system is scientific method and scientific knowledge and that each individual should be left to do what he likes in regard to his moral and spiritual tendencies. As against this, it is being increasingly felt that no education can be complete or even worthwhile if it does not provide to the individual not only the knowledge of the history of moral, religious and spiritual ideas which are a great part of the human heritage but also a non-dogmatic but disciplined process by which the individual is enabled to embody those values which seem to our human thought as indispensable to the survival of human race at the present critical juncture of human history and to the eventual development of a greater civilisation than we have had hitherto. It is, for instance, universally agreed that pursuit of peace is one of the most desirable things that we should encourage in education all over the world.

No body seriously argues that his is a value, which each individual should be left free to pursue or not to pursue and that it should have no place in our educational system. And, we may note that pursuit of peace implies the pursuit of a number of inter-related values such as unity, harmony, mutuality, friendship, faithfulness and sincerity. As a matter of fact, there is in the realm of values an intimate inter-relatedness, and once we admit any given value, we are perforce led to admit the entire range of values.

Nonetheless, it must be admitted that it is not easy to settle the question as to what precise is the relationship between the realm of values and the realm of knowledge, how precisely pursuit of science and pursuit of values should be related to each other, and how precisely we should encourage the pursuit of values in our system of education. There are, however some guidelines that we can derive from the contemporary educational thought and from some of the great educational experiments conducted in India or elsewhere.

In the domain of physical education, the values that we ought to seek are those of health, strength, plasticity, grace and beauty. In the domain of emotional education, the values that we ought to seek would be those of harmony and friendliness, of courage and heroism, of endurance and perseverance and of irresistible will to conquer the forces of ignorance, division and injustice. In the domain of the mental development, the values that we ought to seek would be those of utmost impartiality, dispassionate search after the Truth, Calm and Silence, and widest possible synthesis. The values pertaining to the aesthetic development would be those of the vision of the Beauty and creative joy of the possible aesthetic experience and expression.

Values that we should seek in the moral and spiritual domain are those of sincerity, faithfulness, obedience to whatever one conceives to be the highest, gratitude, honesty benevolence, generosity, cheerfulness, selflessness, freedom from egoism, equality in joy and suffering, in honour and dishonor, in success and failure, pursuit of the deepest and the highest, of the absolute and ultimate and progressive expression of this pursuit in thought, feeling and action.

It would be observed that the pursuit of the above-mentioned values is not intrinsically related to any particular moral or religious doctrine or any particular spiritual discipline. One can pursue these values as something intrinsic and as ends in themselves, irrespective of whether one holds any particular doctrine of ethics, religion or spirituality. Whether one belongs to one religion or the other or to no religion, one can pursue these values devotedly and zealously. This point is extremely important in the context of the Indian situation where there are a number of religions, including atheistic religions, and where there are people of no religion.

This is again important in the context of the fact that our Constitution clearly states that "No religious instruction shall be provided in any educational institution wholly maintained out of the State Fund" and that "No person attending any educational institution recognised by the State or receiving aid out or State Fund shall be required to take part in any religious instruction that may be imparted in such institution or to attend any religious worship that may be conducted in such institution or in any premises attached thereto unless such person or, if such person is a minor, his guardian has given his consent thereto."

A question is often raised as to whether there is any valid distinction between moral and spiritual values. In answer, it may be said that much depends upon what we intend to include in our definition of the word "morality" or in the word "spirituality". In Indian thought, the distinction between morality and spirituality has been clearly made and we have two definite terms, *Naitik and Adhyatmik,* having their specific and distinguishing connotations. The word "morality" connotes a pursuit of the control and mastery over impulses and desires under the guidance and supervening inspiration of a standard of conduct formulated thought in consideration of man's station and duties in society or in consideration of any discovered or prescribed intrinsic law of an deal. Morality is often conceived as a preparation for spirituality. Spirituality on the other hand, begins when one seeks whatever one conceives to be the ultimate and absolute for its own sake unconditionally and without any reserve whatsoever. Moreover, while morality is often limited to the domain of duties, spirituality is fundamentally a search of the knowledge of the highest and the absolute by direct experience and manifestation of this search in every mode living, thinking and acting.

What is called religious, and what in Indian terminology is termed as *Dharmik* is clearly distinguishable from the moral and the spiritual. The differentiate by which religion can be distinguished from morality and spirituality are:

(i) a specific religious belief which is so exclusive that one cannot accept it irrespective of whether one holds that religious belief or any other or none at all;

(ii) every specific religion has, as its essential ingredient, certain prescribed acts, rituals and ceremonies;

(iii) a religious authority to which religious matters are referred and the decision of which is final.

Both moral and spiritual values, particularly those which we have enumerated above, can be practised irrespective of whether one believes in one religion or another or whether one believes in no religion. Both morality and spirituality can be independent of rituals and ceremonies and of any acts specifically prescribed by any particular religion. And both of them are independent of any authority except that of one's own free and direct experience.

Education in moral and spiritual values is quite distinct from "religious instruction." What we are proposing is instruction and training in the entire realm of values-physical, emotional, intellectual, imaginative, aesthetic, moral and spiritual which can be pursued by any individual irrespective of whether he accepts any religion or no religion.

In addition to the values which are enumerated above, value-orientation in education must also include, specifically, those values which are being promoted by UNESCO of which India is a Member-State. This would mean that our educational system should encourage the value of world peace. International understanding and unity of mankind. UNESCO has also put forward through a comprehensive ideal and value, namely, "to be". This ideal has been highlighted in the Report of the International Commission on the development of education, which was constituted by UNESCO in 1971. While explaining the ideal of "To Be", M. Edgar Faure, the Chairman of the Commission, stated that one of the underlying assumptions of the Report is "That the aid of development is the complete fulfilment of man, in all the richness of his personality, the complexity of his forms of expression and his various commitments."

The ideal of "to be" is distinct from the ideal of "to acquire" and "to possess". The ideal of "to be" refers to that direction of effort which leads individual to look deeply within himself and to find in his inner being the source of his varied potentialities and actualities, the source of a harmony of his varied personalities, and the source of a fulfilment is some kind of perfection that transcends egoism and which rests in a vast and integrated self-hood.

It is pertinent to note that the Indian educational thought has constantly emphasised the value of wholeness of integrality and comprehensiveness. In Indian thought, a distinction has been made between the ego and the self, between *Ahambhava and Atman.* According to the Indian thought whereas egoistic personality is ridden with self-contradictions and internal conflicts, the true self-hood is free from these contradictions and conflicts, and it is the integrating centre in which varied personalities are harmonised and integrated personality is thus a recognised ideal that the Indian educational thought has held out as one of the supreme spiritual values. In its fullness, the idea of integrated personality connotes the perfection of a four-fold personality that harmonises wisdom, power, love and skill in works. We, therefore, recommend that the pursuit of this fullness of integrated personality may be regarded as one of the highest values which should be pursued in our educational system.

There are, indeed, certain other values which are uniquely Indian, in the sense that even though these values may be shared by India in common with other countries, they are pursued in India either with a certain special zeal and dedication or pursued with a certain speciality or completeness. For example, the value that we attach to the ideal of tolerance is something special in India. In fact, the word tolerance itself is not adequate to convey the intended meaning in the ordinary idea of tolerance, there is still a feeling that our own preferred idea is somewhat superior to the other contending ideas.

On the other hand, what is peculiarly Indian is the sentiment and the recognition that various principal contending ideas are all equally legitimate ideas and that superiority lies not in holding one idea as one preferred idea but in trying to find such a synthesis that each idea finds its own highest fulfilment in it. It is true that all true tendencies towards synthesis, whether found in Plato or Marx, whether in the West or in the East, have this special characteristic. But what is uniquely Indian is that the value and ideal of synthesis has been pursued throughout the long history of Indian Culture as a most desirable goal—and that too repeatedly and with a very special insistence. A special emphasis should be laid in all our learning process towards the seeking of synthesis not only as an ideal of intellectual development but also as a cherished ideal of Indian culture.

Along with the basic idea of synthesis, there is also the accompanying idea of unity, mutuality and oneness is diversity. That, in spite of there being varying centrifugal forces, there are also supervening powerful and harmonising centripetal forces operating in the Indian life and that the Indian Culture finds its deepest fulfilment not in any exclusive denial but in comprehensive affirmation (or in denial of all denials) need a special empahsis. Our education should be so re-oriented as to give a pre-eminent place to the pursuit of the culture of unity in diversity.

Similarly, what is meant by secularism in the Indian context is uniquely Indian. According to the Western idea, secularism means a tendency or a system of beliefs which rejects all forms of religious faith or worship. It means something that pertains to the present world or to things which are not spiritual or sacred. In the context, however, secularism means comprehensiveness in which all religious receive equal protection, treatment and respect, and in which there is place for every one whether he belongs to one religion or another or to no religion. Again Indian secularism encourages us to approach everything, whether material or spiritual, with a sense of sacredness. In Indian secularism there is freedom for the propagation of each religion without hindrance or bar and there is also the freedom to promote and propagate synthesis of religions. At the same time, Indian secularism insists on the promotion of moral and spiritual values which are common to all religious and to no religion as also on the promotion of a synthesis of science and spirituality. Secularism so defined and understood is thus a very special value that is uniquely Indian.

There are several other Indian values which require a special mention and which should find their right place in our educational system. The sense of joy that is behind various festivals in India which are shared by people of the country is something which can be understood only when one enters into the heart and soul of Indian culture The Indian idea of the rhythm of life and the law of harmony, expressed by the word "Dharma" is also uniquely Indian. The place that India has given to the womanhood and to motherhood, in particular, is again something very unique to India, and which cannot be explained in terms which are current in the world, whether in the context of any orthodox attitude or in the context of what is known as feminism. Again, the value that we attach to the pursuit of knowledge, to the pursuit of purity, to the pursuit of wisdom is something unique, in the sense that these things are valued most and they are cherished most, and on the call of which we are inspired to renounce every thing.

There are indeed certain elements which are Indian, which are basically contradictory of the true Indian spirit, such as casteism, regionalism, and fanaticism. These have, of course, to be rejected, and they should find no place in our educational system. India has always opposed ignorance and division This has been India's dominant theme, and even today, our Indian system of education must declare itself opposed to anything that produces ignorance, superstition and division. It is noteworthy that the great Indian values, became dynamically vibrant during the period of India's struggle for freedom In fact, this period was marked by the rise of great men and women who embodied these values and enriched them. Again, it was during this period that these values guided and shaped great movements and events. Thus a study of our nationalist movement provides us a perennial source of inspiration, and we should lay a special emphasis on this study in our educational system, particularly, in the programmes related to the training of teachers.

TEACHING OF VALUES

There is a profound Indian view about teaching which declares that the first principle of teaching is that nothing can be taught. This paradoxical statement may seem at first sight incomprehensible. But when we look closely into it, we find that it contains significant guidelines regarding the methodology of teaching. It does not prohibit teaching, since it is stated to be the first principle of teaching. It does, however, suggest that the methods of teaching should be such that the learner is enabled to discover by means of his own growth and development all that is intended to be learnt. It points out, in other words, that the role of the teacher should be more of a helper and a guide rather than that of an instructor. This would also mean that the teacher should not impose his views on the learner, but he should evoke within the learner the aspiration to learn and to find out the truth by his own free exercise of faculties.

The truth behind this role of the teacher is brought out by the contention that nothing can be taught to the mind which is not already concealed as potential knowledge in the in-most being of the learner. One is reminded of the Socratic view that knowledge is innate in our being but it is hidden. Socrates demonstrates in the Platonic dialogue, 'Meno', how a good teacher can, without teaching, but by asking suitable questions, bring out to the surface the true knowledge which is already unconsciously present in the learner. As we know, Socrates and Plato distinguished between opinion, on the one hand, and knowledge, on the other. They point out that whereas opinions can be formed on the basis of questionable sense experiences, knowledge which consists of pure ideas is independent of sense-experience and can be gained by some kind of experience which is akin to remembrance. In other words, according to Socrates and Plato, knowledge is "remembered" by a process of uncovering.

Again, according to Socrates and Plato, virtue is knowledge. Therefore, what is true of knowledge is also true of virtue. Just as knowledge cannot be taught but can only be uncovered even so virtue, too, cannot be taught but can be uncovered. But, here again, it does not mean that there is no such thing as teaching or that the teacher has no role to play. It only means that the teacher has to be cognizant of the fact that the learner has in him a potentiality and that this role consists of a delicate and skilful operation of uncovering what is hidden or latent in the learner.

There is, indeed, an opposite view, which is advocated mainly by behaviorists, who maintain that the learner has no hidden potentialities except some rudimentary capacities of reflex responses and that anything and everything can be taught to the learner by suitable processes of conditioning which can be designed according to the goals in view. Thus Watsom claimed that learners can be trained to become whatever you design them to become. According to this view, everything can be taught, all virtues and values can be taught and cultivated by suitable methods of conditioning.

It is not our purpose to enter into a debate with behaviorism. But it is a fact that even behaviorism acknowledges that conditioning presupposes innate reflexes, and that the process of conditioning is dependent upon a reward-punishment system which, whether acknowledged or not, can be explained only if the learner has within him an innate drive towards some kind of goal seeking and fulfilment. In other words, even if we admit that external stimulation and conditioning are effective instruments of learning, it does not mean that stimulation of conditioning could work upon a subject that would be devoid of an innate capacity or drive to respond.

Moreover, the claims of behaviorism have been questioned by several rival theories of psychology. The school of mathematical logic, for example, rejects behaviorism and prescribes that the aim in teaching should be more limited and that the claims as to what can be taught should be more modest. It maintains that the aim of teaching should be to teach procedures and not solutions and that the methods should be so employed that the mental processes are taken in the direction of mathematical logic.

The Gestalt psychology maintains that there are in the learner basic perceptual structures and schemes of behavior which constitute some kind of basic unity. It underlines, therefore, the presence of an innate institution in the learner and it prescribes intuitive methods based on perception, which are found largely in audio-visual pedagogy. Psychoanalysis has discovered an unimaginable large field of innate drives of which our active consciousness is normally unconscious.. But Freudian form of psychoanalysis, which posited eros and thanatos as the two ultimate but conflicting innate drives in man, has been largely over-passed by Adler, Jung and others. Modern psychic research is discovering in the sub-conscious a deeper layer which can properly be termed as subliminal, since it is found to be seat of innate capacities of telepathy, clairvoyance, etc. As psychology is advancing, we seem to be discovering more and more of what is innate in the learner. At the same time, we are becoming more and more conscious of the necessity to be increasingly vigilant about the methods which we should employ in dealing with the learner.

It is, therefore, sometimes argued that there is a valid distinction between knowledge and values and that while knowledge can be taught values cannot be taught. But when we examine this view more closely, we find that what is meant is that the methods which are valid and appropriate in the field of learning in regard to knowledge are not applicable to the field of learning in regard to values.

Corresponding to each domain of learning there are valid and appropriate methods and that the effectivity of learning will depend upon an ever-vigilant discovery of more and more appropriate methods in each domain of learning. It is clear, for example, that while philosophy can be learnt by a process of discussion, swimming cannot be learnt by discussion. In order to learn to swim one has to plunge into water and swim. Similarly, the methods of learning music or painting have to be quite different from those by which we learn mathematics or physics. And indeed, when we come to the realm of values, we must recognise the necessity of a greater scruple in prescribing the methods which can be considered to be distinctively appropriate to this field.

One speciality of the domain of values is that it is more centrally related to volition and affection, rather than to assume that value-oriented education should be exclusively for training of volition and affection. This point needs to be underlined because of two reasons.

Firstly, it is sometimes assumed that value-oriented education should be exclusively or more or less exclusively limited to certain prescribed acts of volition and that the value-oriented learning should be judged by what a learner 'does' rather than what he knows. This is too simplistic and exclusive, and we should avoid the rigidity that flows from this kind of gross exclusivism.

Secondly, and this is an opposite view—it is sometimes argued that learning is primarily a cognitive process and, therefore, value-orientation learning should largely or preponderantly be limited to those methods which are appropriate to cognition. This, too, is a gross exclusivism which should be avoided. While methods appropriate to volition and affection should be more preponderant, methods appropriate to cognition also should have a legitimate and even an indispensable place. This is reinforced by the fact that the striving towards values stirs up the totality of the being and cognition to less than volition and affection is or can be stimulated to its highest maximum degree, provided that the value-oriented learning is allowed its natural fullness.

Instruction, example and influence are the three instruments of teaching. However, in our present system of education, instruction plays an overwhelmingly important role, and often when we think of teaching we think only of instruction. It is this illegitimate identification that causes much confusion and avoidable controversies. If we examine the matter carefully, we shall find that in an ideal system of teaching, instruction should play a much less important role than example and influence of the teacher. It is true that in the domain of learning where cognitive activities play a more dominant part, instruction through lectures and discussions may have, under certain circumstances, a larger role. But in those domains of learning where volitional and affective activities play a larger part, instruction through methods other than lectures and discussions should play a larger role.

In a system of education, where teaching and instruction are almost identified there, is very little flexibility where example and influence can play their legitimate role. Moreover, our present system is a continuous series of instruction punctuated by home-work and tests which accentuate the rigidity of procedure and mechanical adherence to schedule of time-table, syllabi and examinations. In this rigid and mechanical structure, the centre of attention is not the child but the book, the teacher and the syllabus. The methods, which are most conducive to the development of the personality of the child such as the methods of self-learning, exercise of free will, individualised pace of progress, etc., do not have even an elbow room. Indeed, if this is the system of education and if we are to remain content with this system of education, most important elements of learning will for ever remain outside this system, and we cannot confidently recommend any effective system of learning, much less any effective programme of value-education.

Sooner rather than later, our system of education will change in the right direction. An increasing number of educationists and teachers will come forward to break the rigidities of our educational system. Itis possible to make our system more and more flexible And with the right type of training imparted to teachers, a more healthy system of education will eventually be introduced and will become effective.

It is sometimes argued that values can best be taught through the instrumentality of a number of subjects rather than through any specific or special subject, whether we may call it by the name of "moral education" or "ethics", or "value-education". There is a great force behind this contention and a well-conceived programmes of studies of various subjects should naturally provide, both in their content and thrust, the requisite materials for value-education. The question, however, is whether our current programmes of studies have been so carefully devised as to emphasise those aspects which can readily provide to teachers and students the required opportunities, conditions and materials for value-education.

Much work remains to be done before we can give a confident answer in the affirmative. But even if our programmes of studies are revised, there will still remain the specific area of value-education which should receive a special, although not exclusive, attention and treatment. In other words, there should be in the totality of educational programmes a *core programme* of value-education. This core programme should be so carefully devised that various threads of this programme are woven into complex totality of all the other programmes of studies. And yet the central theme of value-education would not form a mere appendage of all other subjects but would stand out at the over-arching and the supervening subject of basic importance.

OUTLINE OF VALUE-ORIENTED EDUCATION PROGRAMME

Education is a vast cycle, and what we propose for one sector of education has repercussions on all the other sectors of education. If we wish our teachers to be value-oriented, it is not merely because we want to tone up our teachers' training programmes. Our teachers should be value-oriented because we want them to be rightly equipped as vehicles of values for the benefit of our children and youth. By this very nature, teacher is a transmitter, a messenger, a carrier. Our determination of what he has to transmit will depend upon what we determine to be valuable for our children and youth. This point has been kept in view while presenting the following outline of a possible programme of value-oriented education which could be treated as a core of totality of the teachers' training programme.

1. Philosophy, Education and Values:

— Man in the Universe: Philosophical views: Indian and Western;

— Aim of Human Life: Varlous views:

— Supra-cosmic, Supra-terrestrial, Cosmic-terrestrial, integral;

— Man's need of progress;

— Progress and Education;

— Aims of Education: Western and Indian themes, UNESCO's ideals and recommendations;

— "Learning to be", The idea of Learning Society;

— Education for International Understanding, Peace and Human Rights;

— Philosophy of New Methods of Education;

— A synoptic view of the recent trends in learning-teaching processes;

— Philosophy of Values;

— Definition of values, moral and spiritual values, aesthetic and emotional values, values of intellectual and physical culture, Ideals of Liberty, Equality, Fraternity, Philosophy of Indian Values.

2. Psychology, Education and Values:

A. Man and Personality;

B. Ego memory and Self: Indian and Western Views. Planes and Parts of the Being: Inconscient, Subconscient, Physical, Vital, Rational, Aesthetic, Ethical, Psychic, Spiritual.

— Multiple Personalities in Man;
— Conflicts within Man;
— Harmonisation of Personalities;
— Freedom from Ego-consciousness;
— Integration of Personality;
— Higher Levels of Personality;
— Multi-dimensional Personality;
— Balanced Personality;
— Personality of Equanimity;
— Four-fold Personality of Wisdom, Power, Harmony and Skill.
— Education of the Body and Values of Physical Culture;
— Education of the Vital and Values of Vital Culture;
— Education of the Rational, ethical and aesthetic being and values of mental culture;
— Education of the in-most being and values of psychic and spiritual culture;
— Concept of Psychological Perfection

Science and Values:

— Nature of Scientific thinking;
— Pursuit of the Value of Truth through Science;
— Science and Self-Knowledge;
— Striking facts revealed by Science;
— Appearance and Reality of Matter;
— Life in Plants;
— Extraordinary Phenomena of intelligence in Birds and Animals;

— The Mysteries of the Human Body;

— Interdependence of Body and Mind;

— Role of Institution in Discoveries and Inventions;

— Idea of the Fourth Dimension;

— Man and Evolution;

— Possibility of Mutation of Species;

— Man and his Mutation;

— Science, Man and Values.

4. Philosophy and Values:

— The Nature of Philosophical Thinking;

— Its distinction from scientific thinking;

— Philosophy and pursuit of the value of Truth;

— Philosophy and the Idea of God;

— Proofs of the Existence of God;

— Attributes of God: Omnipresence, Omniscience, Omnipotence.

Theories of Good and Evil:

(a) Utilitarianism;

(b) Institutionism;

(c) Beyond Good and Evil.

The Problem of Evil, Suffering and Death.

The Problem of Transformation of Human Nature.

5. Religion, Spirituality and Values:

— Selected parables, myths and legends

— Indian Catholicism, Secularism, Tolerance and Synthesis.

— Psychology of Worship and Prayer

— Psychology of Action without Desire

— Psychology of Concentration:

— Meditation and Contemplation.

— Central Spiritual Experience:

— Liberation from the Ego;

— Cosmic Consciousness;

— Transcendental Consciousness;

— Spiritual Transformation;

— Yoga as practical psychology.

— Yoga as Science of Spiritual Experiences;

— System of Yoga;

— Integral Yoga of Sri Aurobindo

— Synthesis of Science and Spirituality

6. Art and Values:

— What is Art?

— Artistic experience: Some Accounts;

— Leonardo Da Vinci, Beethoven,

— Rabindra Nath Tagore.

Art and the pursuit of the Value of Beauty:

Beauty in relation to poetry, music, painting, architecture, dance and drama: some illustrations.

7. Psychological Exercises of Aspiration, Will and Introspectioin as aids to the pursuit of values.

8. Environment and Values

- — Harmony with Nature
- — Love for Vegetable and Animal Kingdom
- — Ecological Balance and Need to protect Earth to receive protection of Earth
- — Eco-development programmes.

9. Works of Community Service, Courage and Heroism

10. Physical Culture and its Values:

(a) Health;

(b) Strength;

(c) Agility;

(d) Grade; and

(e) Beauty.

(f) An Ideal Sportsman

(g) Meaning of Gymnastics, Atheltics, Aquatics, Combatives, Games.

(h) A Daily Programme of Physical Culture.

11. Selected Stories, Plays and Passages of Literature that inspire the pursuit of Truth, Beauty and Goodness:

- — Creation of Educational Environment through Exhibitions, Interior decoration and stimulating atmosphere
- — Lessons of History as an aid to the pursuit of Values;

— Theme of Unity of Mankind in World History.

12. Practical Suggestions and Hints to Teachers

1. The secret of teaching values is to inspire and kindle the quest among the students by means of one's own example of character and mastery of knowledge. It is by embodying values within ourselves that we can really radiate values to our students.

Value-oriented education should not be conceived as an enunciation of a series of Do's and Don'ts The idea of a series of Do's and Don'ts implies a belief that there are certain actions which are absolutely good, and there are others which are absolutely bad. An inner process, however, shows that outer actions derive their value only in relation to the inner motive and the inner consciousness from which those actions emerge. It is not actions in themselves but the inner qualities behind actions which are important. The given right quality may express itself in different forms of actions.. And each of these actions would be right, since behind each one of them there is the living vibration of the right quality. On the other hand, there are several actions which may apparently seem to be good and right in their outer form, and yet, if they are not spontaneous expressions of the right quality, they cease to have any moral and spiritual value.

A good teacher should, therefore, have a sound psychological knowledge of the different parts of the being, of the different qualities that come into play in various actions, and of the right laws of the development of personality in relation to the development of capacities and values of an integrated personality.

Values cannot be taught in the same way as lessons of information. Instruction should form a minor role, and a major role should be assigned to intimate contact and individual guidance. The role of the teacher is to put the child on the right road to his perfection and to encourage him in his growth by watching, suggestions and helping, but not imposing or interfering.

All occassions of daily life should be utilised by the teacher to bring his student nearer to the realisation of the ideals. There are occasions when children express wild impulses and passions, and often they are in revolt. Children have their own daily battles of loyalties and friendship, and there are moments of desperate depression and of violent ethusiasm. There are occasions when children get vexed, become sulky and go on strike. All the occasions are occasions for value-oriented education. With patience and perseverance, the teacher can utilise all these occasions to show the truth and light and to awaken among the children the right sense and the right directions of true progress.

(2) We may now venture to suggest some further guidelines which may be helpful to teachers at different levels of guiding and helping the children:

(a) It may first be noted that a good many children are under the influence of their inner psychic and spiritual being which shows itself very distinctly at times in their spontaneous turning truth, beauty and goodness. To recognise this turning and to encourage it wisely and with a deep sympathy would be the first indispensable step.

(b) The most important quality to develop among the children is sincerity.

(c) This quality and several other qualities are taught infinitely better by example than by beautiful speeches.

(d) The undersirable impulses and habits should not be treated harshly. The child should not be scolded.

Particularly, care should be taken not to rebuke a child for a fault which one commits oneself. Children are very keen and clear-sighted observers: they soon find out the educators' weaknesses and note them without pity.

(e) When a child commits a mistake, one must see that he confesses it to the teacher spontaneously and frankly; and when he has confessed it he should be made to understand with kindness and affection what was wrong in movement and that he should not repeat it. A fault confessed must be forgiven.

(f) A child should be encouraged to think of wrong impulses not as sins or offences but as symptoms of a curable disease which can be remedied by a steady and sustained effort of the will—falsehood being rejected and replaced by truth, fear by courage, selfishness by sacrifice, malice by love.

(g) Great care should be taken to see that unformed virtues are not rejected as faults. The wildness and recklessness of many young natures are only overflowing of an excessive strength, greatness and nobility. They should be purified, not discouraged.

(h) An affection, that is firm yet gentle, sees clearly, and a sufficiently practical knowledge will create bonds of trust that are indispensable for the educator to make the education of a child effective and value-oriented.

(i) When a child asks a question, he should not be answered by saying that it is stupid or foolish, or that the answer will not be understood by him. Curiosity cannot be postponed, and an effort must be made to answer questions truthfully and in such a way as to make the answer comprehensible to the student's mental capacity.

(j) The teacher should ensure that the student gradually begins to become aware of his deeper self and that with this growing awareness the student is able to harmonise and resolve his inner conflicts.

(k) It should be emphasised that if one has a sincere and steady aspiration, a persistent and dynamic will, one is sure to meet, in one way or another, externally by study and instruction, internally by concentration, revelation or experience, the help that one needs. Only one thing is absolutely indispensable, namely, the will to discover and realise. This discovery and this realisation should be the primary occupation of the being, the pearl price which one should acquire at any cost. Whatever one does, whatever one's occupation and activity, the will to find the truth of one's being and to unite with it should always burn like fire behind all that one does, thinks and feels.

(l) At higher levels of development, teacher should use the methods of daily conversation and books read from day to day. Books should contain lofty examples of the past, given not as moral lessons but as things of supreme human interest. These books should also contain (a) great thoughts of great souls, (b) passages of literature which set fire to the highest emotions and promote the highest aspirations, and (c) records of history and biography which exemplify the living of great thoughts, noble emotions and inspiring ideals.

(m) Opportunities should be given or created which would enable students to embody progressively higher and nobler values.

3. There are important aspects of the mental, vital and physical education which contribute to the value-oriented education. They can be briefly mentioned:

(a) In its natural state the human mind is limited in its vision, and narrow in its understanding. It is often rigid in its conceptions, and a certain effort is needed to enlarge it to make it supple and deep. Hence it is very necessary to develop in the child the inclination and capacity to consider everything from as many points of view as possible. There is an exercise in this connection which gives greater suppleness and an elevation to thought. It is as follows:

— A clearly formulated thesis is set; against it is opposed an anti-thesis, formulated with the same precision. Then by careful reflection the problem must be widened or transcended so that a synthesis is found which unites the two contraries in a larger, higher and more comprehensive idea.

— Another exercise is to control the mind from judging things and people hastily and without sufficient data. True knowledge is always at a higher level, and one must be able to reach not only the domain of pure ideas but even of deeper experiences. Therefore, the mind should be trained to be silent and to search deeply in order to drive knowledge from higher regions of pure ideas and deeper experiences.

— One may suggest a further exercise: Whenever there is a disagreement on any matter, as a decision to take, or an action to accomplish, one must not stick to one's own conception or point of view. On the contrary, one must try to understand the other person's point of view, put oneself in his place and instead of quarrelling, find out a solution which can reasonably satisfy both parties. There is always one for men of goodwill.

- A wide, subtle, rich, complex, attentive, quiet and silent mind is a powerful base not only for the discovery of supreme values but also for manifesting them in our outer actions, thoughts and feelings.

(b) The vital being in us is the seat of impulses and desires, of enthusiasm and violence, of dynamic energy and desperate depression, of passions and revolt. The vital being is, however, a good worker, although most often it seeks its own satisfaction. If that is refused totally or even partially, it gets vexed, sulky and goes on strike.

- An exercise at these moments is to remain quiet and refuse to act. For it is important to realise that at such times one does stupid things and can, in a few moments, destroy or spoil what one has gained in months of regular effort.
- Another exercise is to deal with the vital as one deals with child in revolt, with patience and perseverance, showing it the truth and the light, endeavoring to convince it and awaken in it the goodwill.
- A wide, strong, calm but dynamic vital, capable of right emotion, right decision and right execution is an invaluable aid to the realisation of supreme values.

(c) The body of nature is a docile and faithful instrument but it is very often misused by the mind with its dogmas, its rigid and arbitrary principles, and by the vital with its passions, its excess and dissipations. It is these which are the cause of bodily fatigue, exhaustion and disease. The body must, therefore, be freed from the tyranny of the mind and the vital and this can be done by training the body to feel and sense the presence of in-most harmony and peace and to learn to obey its governance.

The emphasis in physical education should be laid on the development of health, strength, agility, grace and beauty through various exercises, whether done by Yogic Asans or by other methods of physical culture such as gymnastics, athletics, aquatics, combatives, games and sports. When the body is rightly trained, it will learn to put forth at every minute the effort that is demanded of it, for it will have learnt to find rest in action, and to replace through contact with universal forces and energies what it spends consciously and usefully. By this sound and balanced practice, a new harmony will manifest in the body, which will give right proportions and the ideal beauty of form.

There are many sports which help to form and necessitate the qualities of courage, hardihood, energetic action, initiative, steadiness of will, rapid decision and action, the perception of what is to be done in an emergency and dexterity in doing it. Another invaluable result of these sports is the growth of the sporting spirit. This includes good humour and tolerance and consideration for all, a right attitude and friendliness to competitors and rivals, self-control and scrupulous observance of the laws of the games, fair play and avoidance of the use of foul means, equal acceptance of victory or defeat without bad humour, and loyal acceptance of the decisions of the appointed judge, umpire or referee. More important still is the custom of discipline, obedience, order and habit of team work which certain games necessitate.

4. *Works of community service should be included as a part of the total educational process. But to make community service truly value-oriented, emphasis should be laid on the true spirit*

with which the proposed work is to be done. Requisite spirit can be developed progressively through certain successive stages. For example, the work inspired by desire or by restlessness should be replaced by the work done with every showing skill and perfection. At the higher stage, work should be done in order to discover its relationship with one's own in-most and highest aspirations. At a still higher level, work should be looked upon as an offering, without any sense of bargain. At still higher stages, work should be done in consonance with the highest ideal that is being progressively worked out in the world, namely, the ideal of solidarity, unity and harmony. The entire discipline of work should be looked upon as *tapasya,* which should be carried out not only in right spirit but also with efficiency and skill. The true morality and spirituality demand meticulous care in handling material things, and one should not tolerate one's own forgetfulness or idleness. There should be a living worship of things, materials, tools and processes of works. There should be an increasing awareness that matter too is sacred.

5. *An important element in children's development is the presentation of dreams of a new world,* a world of peace and international understanding, a world where truth alone would prevail, a world where beauty and goodness would pervade all that we see and experience. Stories and plays to illustrate these dreams would be an effective instrument. Artistic imagination that would refine sensitivity and sense of beauty should develop right from the early stages of education Even ordinary habitual things of daily life should be taught as activities of art and beauty. That even activities such as those of bathing, cleaning the teeth, dressing, sitting and standing require art and refined sense of beauty should be brought home to children and young students. Students should be encouraged to live in harmony with nature and to

develop the habit of clam and intimate company of plants, trees and flowers.

At a little higher stage, students may be introduced to the art of listening to music. Acquaintance with some selected *ragas* (Indian) and harmonies (Western) should be encouraged. Exhibition of books of beauty in its various aspects should also form part of the programmes in schools. A great stress should be laid upon physical fintness as an essential part of the pursuit of beauty. Those who have special interest in music, dance, art and poetry should be given special facilities so that they can develop their interests and capacities in these fields.

Examples of poetic excellence should also be presented to the students in various ways. An idea should be emphasised that just as there is beauty in the harmony of physical forms, even so there is beauty in the harmony of the forms of thoughts, works, feelings and deeds. At a still higher level, special emphasis may be laid on the powers of expression, such as faultless recitation, poetry and dramatics. A special emphasis should be laid on the study of the appreciation of art and music.

A. Since stories play a great role in providing inspiration to the children in regard to values, teachers should prepare various compositions of stories and plays from the world literature which would satisfy at the best the following criteria:

   (i) They should have been written in a language that is chaste and beautiful;

   (ii) They should be full of human interests, which, however, do not involve plots of mischief and cunning; and

   (iii) They should be able to create an atmosphere of peace and harmony and a spontaneous inspiration for Truth, Beauty and Goodness.

B. Teachers should also endeavour to:

(a) Select and compile exercises (i) of remembering and repeating noble aspirations and thoughts, (ii) of observation and accurate descriptions, and (iii) of control of senses and speech and behaviour;

(b) Identify subjects and topics which develop sense of wonder;

(c) identify topics and subjects which would provide an inter-disciplinary study of science and values;

(d) identify activities which may relate to the free choice directed towards control and mastery over lower impulses and towards excellence in studies and in works;

(e) identify topics that would help students to widen and heighten their consciousness;

(f) select topics related to self-knowledge and to the methods of concentration by which human consciousness can be developed not only horizontally but also vertically so as to create states of consciousness in which mutuality, harmony and true brotherhood could flower spontaneously;

(g) identify subjects and topics related to values needed for a new world order of Liberty, Equality and Fraternity; and

(h) finally, identify subjects and topics related to the Values of the Synthesis of the East and the West.

If the teacher is to play his right role in the promotion of value-oriented education, the teacher himself should be value-oriented. It is only when he is himself value-oriented, that he will be able to give the necessary inspiration, help and guidance to his students. Values cannot be taught merely by discourse, just as swimming cannot be taught merely by lecturers. A good teacher of swimming has to be a swimmer himself, and he should be able to take the learner into the waters to make him swim. Similarly, a teacher of values should himself be a seeker and aspirant of values, and he should be ready to walk with the learner on the long and difficult path of realising and embodying values.

10

CHANGING ROLE OF TEACHERS AND METHODS OF TRAINING

It is noteworthy that the role of teacher is sought to be determined during the recent decades, not only in the context of providing the dimension of values in our system of education but also in the context of providing more effective methods of education. These two contexts are not mutually exclusive, and they tend to lead to conclusions that converge upon the important point, namely that the role of the teacher is not merely that of a lecturer.

According to one extreme view, the method of lecturing should be eliminated altogether from our educational system. It has been suggested that teaching should be done through teaching machines or through such devices which involve methods of self-learning.

Against this extreme view, it has been argued that the method of lecturing is indispensable, not as an exclusive method, but as an integral part of the totality of various methods. It has been argued, for instance, that lecturing is a practical demonstration to the students of how a complex and rich mind operates while dealing with a subject in question. It has also been held that lecturers are or can be useful under at least five circumstances, namely,

(a) when a new subject is to be introduced,

(b) when a panoramic view of a given topic or subject is to be presented,

(c) when collective awareness regarding a subject matter needs to be created,

(d) when a discussion on a given problem is sought to be stimulated and conducted and

(e) when some general information is to be provided for any collective purposes.

It has also been urged that lectures are effective instruments when results of a recent research or discovery are to be communicated, particularly, when no written material is as yet available. Finally no one seriously disputes the tremendous value of an inspired speech, particularly when it flows from profundities of knowledge and experience.

At the same time, it has now come to be increasingly realised that the most essential and indispensable role of the teacher is to try to understand his students and to help each one in his growth and development. In this view, the first thing that the teacher should do is to observe his students at work and at play, with deep insight and sympathy. The second step should be to provide to the whole group of his students as also to each member of the group the necessary stimulus in the right direction. This stimulus could be in the form of a lecture or in the form of a conversation or a suggestion or a demonstration or a general or initial remark. That a given teacher should be a good lecturer is understood, but it is increasingly felt that he should also be capable of formulating short and striking words and ideas which can be communicated briefly and effectively. He should also be capable of knowing when a personal or individual explanation to a given student would be useful and fruitful. There are occasions when silence is more eloquent than a speech. And, above all, the teacher should, by his own enthusiasm and his own uplifting example, provide, a stimulating atmosphere that would inspire his students to work, joyously and eagerly towards excellence.

It is admitted that these are difficult things, and that we are led to demand a great deal from the teacher. But it is argued that the changes that are coming over the entire human race, and the exigencies of the crisis through which mankind is passing today impose upon us an imperative to demand from our teachers qualities and capacities which are not so common. It is therefore urged that teachers have to play roles which are largely new and which are admittedly difficult.

The International Commission on the Development of Education, established by UNESCO, submitted its report in 1972 under the title: *Learning To Be.* In this report, certain far-reaching recommendations have been made in regard to teachers and teachers' training programme. It has been, for example, pointed out: "One of the essential tasks of educators at present is to change the mentalities and qualifications inherent in all professions; thus they should be the first to be ready to rethink and change the criteria and basic situation of the teaching profession, in which the job of educating and simulating students is steadily superseding that of simply giving instructions."

It has been further pointed out that the present day divisions between formal and informal, school and out-of-school, child and adult education are steadily fading. It has, therefore, been recommended that the conditions in which teachers are trained should be profoundly changed so that, essentially, they become educators rather than mere specialists in transmitting pre-established curricula. It has been underlined that the teaching profession will not be in a position to fulfil its role in the future unless it is given, and develops itself, a structure better adapted to modern educational systems.

Widespread and efficient use of new technologies in education is possible only if sufficient change takes place within the system itself. It has, therefore, been recommended that teacher training programmes should be so modified that teachers are equipped for the different roles and functions imposed by new technologies.

The qualities, capacities and skills that we should aim at among teachers should include:

(a) A spontaneous but well-cultivated interest in observing students with deep insight and sympathy;

(b) Psychological tact to deal with collective and individual needs of growth of students;

(c) Capacity to lead students to the art of self-learning;

(d) A cheerful and enthusiastic disposition capable of inspiring students to pursue values and excellence with sincerity and dedication;

(e) Capacity of guiding and counselling, more by suggesting and by uplifting example rather than by lecturing;

(f) Capacities not only for a formal education but also for non-formal and informal education;

(g) Capacity to handle self-learning equipment, audio-visual instruments and various kinds of new learning materials including work sheets, workbooks, programmed books, test papers with auto-correcting components and other materials required for vocational guidance;

(h) Knowledge of art and science of educating the personality in all its aspects with a special emphasis on integration, harmony and excellence.

As a practical measure, the methods which are currently employed in the teachers' training institutions should be so changed that the trainees would have the opportunity of first hand experience of new methods and techniques of learning during their training programmes.

A working model that could be suggested may be described as follows:

(a) Teachers under training should at the outset be provided with a document explaining the new roles for the teachers as also various new methods and techniques involved in the learning-teaching process.

(b) Trainees would be required to indicate their willingness to employ new methods of learning in their own training;

(c) Trainees would then be advised to study their various subjects, as far as possible, through the process of self-learning;

(d) Educators of the trainees would be available for consultation as and when needed, for shorter or longer duration, by prior appointment, or at certain hours of the day, without any prior appointment;

(e) Educators would deliver lectures from time to time, as and when necessary, but these lectures would be much fewer than in the ordinary system of education;

(f) Educators would combine lectures with seminars, tutorials, demonstrations, exhibitions and individualised guidance so as to make the process of training as effective as possible;

(g) Each trainee would undertake a project, the report of which would, at the end of the training period, indicate his pursuit of excellence and values which are sought to be promoted through the training programme;

(h) The training institution should provide opportunities and facilities to the trainees to handle audio-visual equipment, new learning-teaching material, work sheets, programmed books, teaching machines and other latest instruments meant for individualised learning as also for various other methods which are sought to be employed in new emerging models of teaching-learning;

(i) Educators in the training institutions would devote themselves to extending to the trainees the necessary help, guidance, counsel and inspiration;

(j) Education would give to the trainees individualised tests from time to time, as and when necessary, with a view to giving opportunities to the trainees:

   (a) to revise what they have studied;

   (b) to ascertain the degree of proficiency achieved;

   (c) to stimulate and encourage them to study further; and

   (d) to develop new interest and new lines of studies;

(k) A record of progress would be maintained by each trainee in which he will record, among other things, books read and results achieved at various tests.

In order that the candidate is free to direct his own training programme he should be free to take or not to take any particular test during the training programme, except when in the view of the educators he is unable to use his freedom intelligently and prudently and is therefore in need of compulsory compliance with the advise and directions of the educators.

At the end of the training period, the candidates would have the possibility of taking a Public Examination, provided that he obtains from the head of the training institution a testimonial that he has shown during the training period qualities of regularity, punctuality and diligence in work as also disciplined behaviour.

- — The Public Examination should consist of a written test and an oral test.
- — The written test will consist of at least four papers. Of these, one paper will cover the programme that has been suggested as the core programme of value-oriented education.
- — The second paper would pertain to achievements of Indian Culture, National struggle for freedom, ideals of Liberty, Equality an Fraternity, and the theme of Unity of Mankind.
- — The next two papers would pertain to any combination of subjects that the student might have chosen to specialise in.

In the oral test, each interviewee would have the opportunity to explain the report of the project that he might have submitted earlier, on completion of the training period. In addition, the interviewee will be tested in respect of the depth of knowledge of subjects of his specialisation as also in respect of the general attainments of the development of personality and dedication of serious thought and to high ideals. The interview should be of a duration of at least half an hour.

One of the serious maladies of the written tests is that of cheating practised by a number of students. Various suggestions have been made to cure this malady. Some suggestion to arrange the written tests are listed below:

(a) There should be a question bank in every concerned library where a number of questions pertaining to various topics of studies could be available.

(b) Students should be free to get themselves acquainted with the questions pertaining to their own subjects and topics.

(c) In the examination hall, a selection from the totality of these questions, classified subject-wise (and topic-wise, if necessary) should be available.

(d) These questions would be printed on a specially designed paper, each question on a separate slip on one side only. The other side of the slip would be blank and slip would be so folded that only the blank side would be visible from outside.

(e) Each student would be permitted to pick up any questions by lot, and he would be expected to answer any four or five of these questions.

(f) For every question, there would be separate answer sheet, and at the commencement of the answer, the student would be required to paste the question slip.

(g) Thus, every student will have a separate set of questions, and there would be no possibility of leakage or of cheating.

Candidates who would be declared successful at this Public Examination would be entitled to appointment, on a competitive basis, to a teaching post in any secondary school. He will similarly be entitled to appointment in any higher secondary school, provided that he has the requisite post-graduate qualification as well.

TASKS OF TEACHERS

Consideration of the teacher's role becomes somewhat abstract in the background of the unpleasant reality that although there is in our country a large army of teachers and a sizeable number and variety of institutions for professional training of the teachers, there is no 'profession' of teaching as such indicative of what the teachers stand for and what responsibility the profession professes to own for itself. It spite of more than three decades of independence, the authoritarian control, characteristic of the sad imperial times, still prevails and the teacher is told what he must do and how to do what he must. He is not expected to have a mind of his own and he is only marginally involved, if at all, in decision making relating to goals, means administration and organisation of education all of which is done for him by others and done remotely.

The teacher is expected merely to obey; teach what he is asked to teach; teach those pupils in the selection of whom he has had little choice; limit his teaching to the books and courses prescribed; train pupils in his charge to pass examinations which are held and evaluated by others and finally be judged and rewarded by standards which have hardly any concern with his professional conscience. His task is more or less mechanical and he must carry out instructions conveyed to him by the grand machinery of education consisting of boards of education, universities, government departments and others.

Professional idealism, professional morality, professional conscience, professional standards of behaviour and, in brief, the professional spirit, does not grow in vacuum of professional responsibility and involvement in relevant decision-making relating to education. It would sound cruel but it is not for wrong to say that the teachers constitute only a large labour force for building education as best technicians and mechanics but not builders, designers and architects. This would be evident from the major concerns expressed by our teachers' organisations and associations, which are not unlike those of other labour organisations in respect of manner of expression which is not invariably elegant and dignified as well as of substance of demands which hardly goes beyond the size of the pay packets and personal benefit. It is sometimes asked, would it matter to education at all, if professional training such as is imparted at present to the various categories of teachers is withdrawn? It would not be pure cynicism to answer that some good money will be saved and education will be spared much unmerited damage that is being done to it by the formality of training required only to meet the regulations governing selection of professional staff.

The freedom allowed by the states to the higher echelons of the teaching profession, which are excused formal profession education, has also not been used for cultivation of professional spirit nor the imperative need of the present time in our country is to create conditions necessary for cultivation of refined professional personality and life-style for the teacher worthy of his responsibility and dignity as an inspirer, and, to no small extent, as a fashioner of the human destiny. Teacher is too low nor too high in the hierarchy of the profession to be denied the elevating experience.

The image of the teacher varies from time to time, country and cultural traditions of different races and seems to be influenced to no small extent by the prevailing conditions and problems of life, vital to the individual and the community. Expectations from the teacher differ and even conflict. Sparta, of old, was intolerant of the weaklings who were better left to perish unlamented; only the strong and able were to be made stronger and abler. This attitude contracts with the distrust of talent expressed by the unimaginative devotees of democracy as well as, on the other extreme, with the contemporary human concern for the mentally and physically handicapped.

We still entertain administration for some of the stern but genuinely good hearted teachers who believed that education was best imparted through the rod, the neglect of which was equated with unbecoming softness and professional irresponsibility. This picture differs widely from some of the contemporary permissive attitudes which encourage primrose-pathing and even dalliance and suffer anarchical out-bursts and destructive actions of the pupils as legitimate expression of protest against the failings of the ruling generation.

In our own country, we cherish nostalgically the idyllic picture of the ashrams of our "rishis" located in secluded forests, "far from the madding crowds ignoble strife," where the teacher and the taught shared, alike, the chores of life as well as lofty philosophy. To live in the ashrams, the wallless institutions; to live with nature and to sit at the feet of the master and watch him live and work and think was considered to be the best of education.

Behind the seeming differences in the role of the teacher in various societies, some common attitudes are discernible. One such feature relates to the culture of the people which the teacher is expected to communicate to the new generation along with its hopes and fears. In open societies with liberal traditions, culture is not forced down the throats of the pupils.

The teacher is free to interpret culture and its significance to the contemporary problems of life and to allow criticism by students of its various aspects and implications. The pupils are not expected to accept cultural attitudes of the past as a creed but they have to be aware of the ripe thinking of the past generations on problems which have mattered to life of the people and to its happiness. In other societies where the needs of education are confined to the ends of the state, the options for the teacher are restricted and he is expected to be a conformist and to indicate in the minds of the pupils dogmatic acceptance of political ideologies for theological doctrines advocated by the leadership in power.

There are also societies which have recently recovered freedom after long periods of political and cultural domination where there is a kind ambivalence because of cultural alienation. Unsure of their identify, the people tend to be eclectic and view their problems as outsiders would view them, that is, with little emotion and sense of involvement. It takes time to get over the mental attitudes to which people get accustomed through generations of educational and cultural influences and it requires no small courage to look at things afresh. Even if it means mounting a big effort, it is necessary that the process of self-examination and self-determination which are essential to all cultures, should begin and continue vigorously.

There are teachers and teachers. Socrates crusaded against the sophists of his time who taught the youth to be clever and to learn effective rhetoric to gain popular applause by making the worse appear the better reason.. Fagin, character of Dickens, taught small urchins the fine art of pick pocketing. We have teachers who teach wrestling, cricket, judo, karate and other sports. We also have teachers who teach music, painting, manual skills, workshop practice, agricultural operations and other arts and crafts necessary for making money and earning a livelihood.

But the working 'teachers' do not refer to those who train pupils merely for making a living—not as it is sometimes said for "preparing slaves to a machine or to an office or to a single money making skill." It is true that a teacher with a vision can give liberal orientation to instruction in any special skill or vocation. The word teacher, however, refers to those who impart education fitted for a free man, free to order his life according to his well-conceived thoughts and philosophy of life, free from whatever social and other pressure which inhibit or compel the mind of man.

Education for freedom is inspiration for continuous initiative to growth from within to full and prudent utilisation of all abilities of a person, that is, in other words, to self-realisation. Education of a free person lies in his appreciation of his role, relationship and responsibility to the physical and social environment in which he is cast, and at the same time experiencing of the deeper awareness within him that while he is in the world he is not of it. He may find himself caged in a body, impelled by the baffling powers of the mind and circumstanced by time and space; but nevertheless; he is still free, if he chooses to be so to explore his spiritual essence. The teacher is bound by a curriculum and he must teach subjects which he is called upon to teach; but most powerful influence of his personality lies in 'the hidden curriculum' of his personality and silent message which is excluded by his way of thinking, discipline of mind and refinement of tastes. A man is what he loves and cares for.

A teacher must no doubt teach certain subjects. The purpose is not merely to impart knowledge of the subject and help to train the mind of the pupil in the discipline of thinking characteristic of the subject and to apply what he learns to what he needs. He is expected to relate what he teachers, through processes of formal and non-formal instruction, to the wider objectives of education, viz. cultivation of spirit of independent enquiry and sensitiveness to moral obligations and good tastes. Moral values have bearing on the context of social life and human relationship.

Social history is a continuing experiment, often silent and unconscious; but sometime deliberate and violent, for adjustment between individual and social growth. It happens sometimes that a society striving for security and survival in the internationally competitive communities and maximisation of economic efficiency tends to exercise strangle-hold on the individual and dwarf his personality.

Strange phenomena sometime overtake the people - senseless struggle for power leading to wars, oppression of the weak, threats unleashed by piling of nuclear and other weapons of destruction; development of industries in some countries with consequent economic enslavement of the less developed countries; defilement of environment and massacre of forests, these and other fears exercise the minds of the thinking people. The teacher must ever be alert and watch out what may affect the future of humanity. The future is before him in the classroom; in the youth under his tutelage. His main concerns would obviously be to strive to cultivate interests and skills necessary for responsible evaluation of the social and human context and abilities to formulate judgements and provide correctives necessary to remove prevailing imbalances with a view to enabling full freedom for growth both for the individual and the society and to preserve the society from the threatening ills.

The teacher should therefore learn to appreciate and evaluate the context of the contemporary social life and the factors that condition it. He should also learn to invite and encourage pupils to contemplate in a detached, dispassionate and objective manner on the social trends of his times and to have visions of life as ideally lives as well as of effective and peaceful methods of social change. In order to be able to perform this function satisfactorily, the teacher has to be well-informed of the currents and cross-currents, historical and ideological, which influence life. The teacher should cultivate silent, sober, and serene detachment to sense what ails the individual and the society and to read the writing on the wall and to appreciate where humanity is drifting to.

In most of the schools the teacher is in contact with his pupils during the school or college working hours—five or six hours. After these school hours the educational process does not come to a stop nor does the pupil hybernate. In fact, more-compelling and alluring and indeed more effective processes of education or miseducation keep operating in the world outside the school. The environment, natural and at home and outside, keeps shaping the mind of the young. There was never any time a choice between 'education' and 'no-education', for to live itself is education. It was said at one time that to live in the Athens of Pericles was the best of education. The choice always is between 'bad' education and 'good' education.

At no time in the history of mankind, the forces of communication technology—the film, radio, TV, the newspaper—keep influencing the mind all the time. The hypnotic orator of deception has been perfected by politicians. The conduct of many of our leaders and functioning of social and political institutions do not go unnoticed by the youth. Blatant corruption and its callous tolerance; low means and shortcuts to power and wealth; the manner in which civic and political institutions are run; the way the government offices and officers function; the devices by which elections are fought and positions of power gained; these and several other factor exercise influence on the youthful minds and they are some times reflected and rehearsed in the elections to the college/university unions and the perpetual war against the university authorities.

Increasing instances of brutal violence, tardy justice, all too concerned for natural justice to the culprit and totally unconcerned for any justice to the wronged, robbed and slaughtered, seem to make the youth feel that laws an made to defeat justice. These and other factors build in the minds of the youth a moral attitude and encourage permissiveness. The youth is intelligent enough to realise what deliberate misuse of some otherwise unexceptional concepts—democracy, socialism, liberty of expression, rights of minorities and weaker sections of society, and other similar concepts is made for the benefit of a few and the worst crimes are committed in the name of social and political catchwords. Dostoevsky repeatedly warned against playing irresponsibly with abstract ideas, e.g. democracy, socialism, liberty, equality and so on—because 'ideas have consequences'. There is enough experience of how these good concepts are used and what strage ends they are made to serve. Whitehead pointed out that great ideas enter reality in strange disguises and disgusting alliances. Roszak draws attention to the vexing paradoxes of modern industrial and technological age, viz. that intensified progress seems to be bound up which intensified unfreedom and thanks to communication technology, irrationality acquires character of rationality.

It is in this background that the teacher is expected to keep himself vigilant and provide models of sobriety and cool observation and thinking. Never before the task of the teacher was more challenging nor was he expected to wage of longer struggle with himself to keep his poise, clarity of vision and sobriety of judgement. This self-discipline on the part of the teacher cannot be taken for granted; he had to be given opportunities for learning to exercise self-discipline to keep him cool in the bewildering phenomenon of life. Neitzche compared an educated person to a tight rope walker; all the drum beating and noises, and the jostling of the crowds around him would not disturb his balance. This virtue cannot be imparted through formal classroom instruction. If the teacher has it, the pupil will hopefully have it.

Tradition is said to bring to teachers respect of the pupil and the society alike; but this tradition has received shocks in recent times and the teachers cannot take respect for granted. He has to earn in the hard way and to merit it. His scholarship and sincerity of purpose would no doubt command respect; but the teacher is not invariably expected to be bright. Only a few teachers are bright. His real influence lies in what he is and what he makes of himself.

The teacher's influence is not confined to what he does during his teaching hours in the classroom; in reality he teaches all the time. He is constantly watched by hundred of pairs of eyes; the way he walks and talks, studies and prepares his lessons; conducts himself inside and outside the classroom; the company he keeps; his habits of living, thinking and studying the way he treats his family and employees and all that he does is watched. The teacher lives in a glass house; he has hardly any private life. He is the observed of all observers and what he does tends unconsciously to be mimicked by the students.

The teachers thus provide models—good or bad—of behaviour for the pupils. Mimickry is the silent tribute the pupil pays to the teacher. This imposes on a teacher responsibility which is in some way unique. Educational literature sometimes refers to 'man-making', as one major concern of teacher education. Whatever may be understood by the term 'man-making', the more important function of teacher education should be to provide environment, inspiration, opportunities and all these are necessary to help the teacher to 'make himself', in other words, to cultivate his personality and to realise the best he is capable of. He has to learn to mould his life-style, his habit of walking, talking, laughing, working, thinking and conducting himself in public or private life.

The most valuable and enduring influence of a teacher a lies in the silent power of example. In ancient India the pupil lived with the teacher in sylvan hermitage in an atmosphere of solitude and silence. The pupil watched his teacher and imbibed the inward methods of the functioning of the teacher's mind, the secrets of his efficiency, the sources of his insprings of happiness, and the spirit of his life and world.

A disciplined teacher, correct and orderly in his habits, sensitive to the needs of those less fortunate in life, gracious and magnanimous; in his dealings with those around him, unruffled by the storms that blow around him, unwilling to stoop to whatever is mean and low however gainful it may be, always cheerful and pleasant without being vulgar and boisterous, will influence much better than through eloquent lectures. Whether in performance in any situation, the power of the teacher's will and his resolute defiance of difficulties constitute education which no formal teaching can provide.

The teacher must learn to acquire faith in himself. It is not less important that he should have faith in his student and in his capacity to develop all his powers and to build up his individual personality. One malady that characterises the educational system at present is the practice of passing judgements on the students and declaring them good or bad, worthy or unworthy, successful or unsuccessful. This is followed up by hero-worship and special rewards for those who are declared successful and even unconscious disincentive for those declared failures. Judgements of this kind must stop.

The teachers should appreciate that traditionally accepted educational methods inhibit full growth of man and create artificial values for evaluation of human spirit. It may even be said that the present system of evaluation in the system of education defeats full growth of man and develoment of several valuable human qualities. It is no wonder that some men who fortunately missed education achieved great heights in various levels.

The world was not lacking in great and good men before the system of schooling came into being. It is no wonder that thinkers like Iwan llich suggest de-schooling of society. The achievements of the school are not only limited but tend to create wrong human values. The teacher, therefore, must learn to adopt a wider view of education and desist from the practice of passing judgement on the student on the basis of schools and examination records. He would err on the right side if he assumes that there can be wrong syllabus, wrong curriculum, wrong textbooks, everything wrong, but not wrong pupil. Teacher's faith in the pupil and his endeavour to help him to discover himself is real education. It is the teacher's responsibility to understand his pupil independently of the customary categorisation fashionable in the system of education.

There is at present a growing concern for helping the student to acquire social skills and relevant knowledge which would enable the pupil to live in a society which is getting more and more complex and to participate in the social, economic and political process that affects its destiny. Participation in social and national life and cultivation of human attitudes and sense of social justice and respect for other persons' point of view are no doubt essential parts of proper education. It is equally important for the teacher to appreciate that a man has also to live with himself and he cannot run away from himself. The most important things happen to man in solitude. The most important decision are taken, new discoveries are made, and novelties perceived in the loneliness of the mind.

The teacher must have a philosophy of his own which should be reflected in his behaviour; but he would be misunderstood if he confined himself to airy abstractions. He must also be a down-to-earth realist and his sense of realism should be reflected in his relationship with the subjects he teaches. It would be sad if the pupil got the impression that the teacher teaches certain subjects only because he is hired and paid for it and that he is no better than any other mercenary. Such a teacher may enable the student to pass an examination, but he will command little respect. What affects the students' mind and attitude is the devotion of the teacher to his subjects and his genuine involvement in its development. His seriousness in his studies and in struggling with the many problem arising out of it, his joy in discovery of novelty in the course of his studies become infectious for his pupils.

The teacher who merely repeats a laboratory experiment mechanically and purposelessly as a matter of prescribed drill, the teacher who teaches geography and astronomy without looking out or gazing at the skies at night, the teacher who teaches history out of books and is uninterested in local history and ancient monuments, will not kindle fire in the minds of the pupils. He should not be surprised if he gets a cold reception from his class. The enthusiasm and commitment of the teacher to his subject and his ability to inspire and arouse interest in the minds of the students determines the quality of the teacher.

The teacher must also be aware of the best known methods of teaching the subjects he teaches and he should learn those methods by practising them. But he should be a master of methods and not a blind follower of the fashionable ones. Methods of teaching are experiments the results of which need constant watching. Methods need to be refined continually in the light of the results achieved. Methods are personal and depend largely on the teacher's concept of what he aims to do and his imaginative approach to putting his ideas across to the pupil in order to inspire him to learn. The teachers must be constantly aware of the methods used by other teachers and also testing the methods of teaching he adopts.

The teacher is a communicator. He communicates through spoken and written words, his voice, his language and choice of words; his actions while speaking, contribute to his effectiveness. His pen-manship, handwriting, elegant arrangement of written work, reflect his efficiency. The teacher communicates himself through his work and deftness in handling material and performance of skilled work. Slopiness and carelessness on his part does not remain unnoticed. The teacher has also to acquire knowledge of skills in use of teaching aids and gifts of modern educational technology such as audio-visual aids e.g. educational films, filmstrips and closed-circuit TV sets, use of computers, language laboratories and programmed learning techniques and the like. Above all, the teacher must be able to improvise and innovate with the help of whatever opportunities are locally available. He should never be at a loss.

BIBLIOGRAPHY

Beyer, Landon E.. et al. (1989). *Preparing Teachers as Professionals.* New York: Teachers College Press.

Broderick, Maria. (ed.) (1988). *For Teachers about Teaching.* Harvard Educational Review. Cambridge.

Burke, Peter. (1987). *Teacher Development: Induction, Renewal, and Redirection.* Falmer Press. New York.

Cochran-Smith, M., & Zeichner, K. (2005). *Studying Teacher Education: The Report of the AERA Panel on Research and Teacher Education.* Mahwah, NJ: Lawrence Erlbaum.

Curriculum Framework for Quality Teacher Education (1998) NCTE, New Delhi.

Dunkin, Michael J. (1987) *International Encyclopedia of Teaching and Teacher Education.* Pergamon Press. Oxford.

Government of India, Teacher Education in Five Year Plans, (1951-97), Planning Commission, New Delhi.

Heimbecker, C., Miner, S., & Prater, G. (2000). Community-Based Native Teacher Education Programs. In J. Reyhner, J. Martin, L. Lockard, & W. Gilbert (Eds.), Learn in Beauty: Indigenous Education for a New Century (pp. 35-44).

Manuelito, K. (2003). *Building a Native Teaching Force: Important Considerations.* Washington, DC: Office of Educational Research and Improvement.

N.K. Venkateswaran. (2003). *On Teaching.* The National Council for Teacher Education. New Delhi.

National Curriculum for Teacher Education; A Framework (1988), Department of Teacher Education, NCERT, New Delhi.

Pearson, Allen T. (1989). *The Teacher: Theory and Practice in Teacher Education*. Routledge. New York.

Peters, R.S. (1977). *Education and the Education of Teachers*. Routledge. London.

Postman, N. (1969). *Teaching as a Subversive Activity*. Doubleday, New York.

Report of NCTE Committee for Teacher Education Programme Through Distance Education Mode (1990), Department of Teacher Education, NCERT, New Delhi.

Special Orientation Programme for School Teachers (SOPT) (1994-97), NCERT, New Delhi.

Teacher Training Agency.(2001). *The Use of ICT in Subject Teaching—Expected outcomes of the New Opportunities Fund ICT training initiative for teachers in England, Wales and Northern Ireland*. Teacher Training Agency: London.

UNESCO. (2001). UNESCO Report: *Teacher Education Through Distance Learning: Technology-Curriculum-Cost-Evaluation*. UNESCO.

University Grants Commission (1995), B.Ed. Through Correspondence for Inservice Teachers (Takwale Committee), UGC, New Delhi.

INDEX